NITTY GRITTY FOODBOOK

NITTY GRITTY FOODBOOK

A Compendium of
Basic Foods for Earthy People

Sheryll Patterson Herdt

Original drawings by Beth Hay

PRAEGER PUBLISHERS
New York

Published in the United States of America in 1975
by Praeger Publishers, Inc.
111 Fourth Avenue, New York, N.Y. 10003

Library of Congress Cataloging in Publication Data

Herdt, Sheryll Patterson.
  Nitty gritty foodbook.

  Bibliography: p.
  1. Food.   2. Cookery.   3. Organic farming.
1. Title.
TX355. H47   641.3   73-10918
ISBN 0-275-51440-4
ISBN 0-275-63310-1 (pbk.)
Jacket and cover design by Beth Hay

Printed in the United States of America.

This book is dedicated to my father,
Lannon Samuel Patterson,
humanist and farmer, who lives
in my memory, and to my mother,
Marian Patterson Haltom,
nitty gritty homemaker

The author's profits from this book go toward the
development of Nitty Gritty Farm, an organic homestead
associated with the Eco-Energy Farm Community.
Nitty Gritty Farm will eventually operate entirely on
nonpolluting, renewable alternative sources of energy,
particularly wind, sun, and methane.
The author welcomes your correspondence,
directed through her publisher.

CONTENTS

ACKNOWLEDGMENTS

The energy needed to create this book came from many people. My sincere thanks go to all, noted or unnoted, who contributed in any way.

Back in the beginning, my mother, Marian Patterson Haltom, taught me about food, and my grandmother Katherine Mohrlang taught her. At the side of my father, Lannon Patterson, I learned about animals and gardening. I had a great desire to bring knowledge about food and self-sufficiency to the people of the new age, and the Community Free School of Boulder, Colorado, provided the medium. Then my students and family and friends encouraged me to write the original edition. Ron Herdt offered moral, technical, and financial support. Tim, Julie, and Greg Herdt, who like to eat, encouraged me to learn these things in the first place, and now that they've grown older, they cook and offer suggestions. I thank my animals, Sukie, Fritz, Shaman, Valentine, Sally, and all the others for teaching me and for eating my mistakes!

The debts for this edition are numerous. For transmission of my ideas, I thank Ruth and Judith Goode. They not only believed in me, but saw the path. At Praeger, Cherene Holland and David Bell were tremendous. I never knew people in publishing to be so pleasant, so helpful, so sensitive. My illustrator, Beth Hay, not only does exquisite drawings, but also helps milk my goats. To my readers who write to me, I am indebted.

But my greatest debt of all is one of the heart—to those dear friends who gave me what I needed most—themselves, their energy, their love, their encouragement. Thus, my deepest thanks to Charles George, Sharon Niederman, Walt Black, Neal Patterson, Suzy Braithwaite, Jon Glazer, and Ron Herdt for helping me, for believing in me, for loving me, and most of all, for bringing me joy and laughter.

This book is yours as well as mine.

NITTY GRITTY
FOODBOOK

INTRODUCTION

The room was packed and overflowing with all kinds of people—a melting pot of the so-called generation/lifestyle/sex gaps. A young man with long hair in a ponytail sat next to an elderly white-haired woman in a pink housedress. A nursing mother in jeans sat beside a woman with a beauty-shop coiffure and tailored suit. About half the students were men and half were women. They talked together and gradually warmed to each other. They were excited and anxious to learn.

The occasion was "Nitty Gritty Foods," a class I taught for several years in the Community Free School at Boulder, Colorado. I had originally offered the class to keep some of the traditional food ways from dying, and to blend them with the new.

Yet the response by both men and women, young and old, was overwhelming. This artform was clearly alive and well. Organic food enthusiasts, back-to-the-landers, those desirous of self-sufficiency, those discontented with overpriced "convenience" foods were anxious for the knowledge. All were eagerly seeking a better life style. Classes were always filled and registration closed before everyone could be included.

Those classes were the birthing of this book. My phone rang often, and people stopped by with questions as they began to experiment with foods themselves. Finally, I couldn't fill the requests in person, so I wrote the original edition of *Nitty Gritty Foods* in 1971 because the information my students sought was not available in one concise volume, and sources were sometimes hard to locate. This book answers the questions they asked most often.

Much of my information was passed on to me by my mother and grandmother while I was growing up on a Nebraska farm in the 1940's. Years later, as my own family started its gradual move from the suburbs back to the land and the basics, I found myself searching my memory for tidbits of information. I returned to speak with relatives and other older people in the Midwest. I developed some of my own methods and searched through numerous books and pamphlets for original methods. It was difficult because most of the books available today simply do not begin with the basics. They presume the processed supplies come from the grocery store.

This book is for you if you'd like to begin at the beginning with food. It will help you become familiar with eating for economy, for health, and for pleasure. I'll stress basic nutrition and organic foods and the most expedient methods to obtain a good balance of both. But I'm not a purist; I'm a nitty gritty cook.

Most of the foods in this book are amazingly inexpensive. And most are suited to both city and rural living. We'll discuss making bread, butter, and jams; cereals like Familia and granola; yogurt and sourdough; methods of preserving fruits, vegetables, and meats. You'll learn how to garden and care for small livestock if you want to obtain your food supply from the original sources. This material is a combination of both old and new ways of nitty gritty living.

These methods are not necessarily how you should do it, but rather how I do it—a guide for you. If you learn enough about the basics of foods, you'll develop some of your own ways. You'll learn when you have a free artistic hand with foods and when you must follow specific directions.

Nitty Gritty Foodbook gives information not readily available in most cookbooks. At the back you'll find a comprehensive bibliography for suggested further reading of related materials, and a list of sources of items that are difficult to find.

FOODCRAFT

"The one absolutely essential requirement for the art of cooking is a love for its raw materials: the shape and feel of eggs, the sniff of flour, or mint, or garlic, the marvelous form and shimmer of a mackerel, the marbled red texture of a cut of beef, the pale green translucence of fresh lettuce, the concentric ellipses of a sliced onion, and the weight, warmth, and resilience of flour-dusted dough under your fingers. The spiritual attitude of the cook will be all the more enriched if there is a familiarity with barns and vineyards, fishing wharves and dairies, orchards and kitchen gardens."—Alan Watts, "Murder in the Kitchen," from *Does It Matter?* (Vintage Books, 1970).

Eating is one of the things we creatures do with regularity, if we are fortunate. While some parts of the world today have little choice in kind and quantity of food, we have vast resources. Yet we don't know the proper ways to use our food. We have lapsed into laziness and carelessness as a society, with many foods coming precooked, prepackaged, and all but predigested. And they are also high in cost.

We do this for the sake of "saving time," but we rarely do. For all the time we spend in grocery store lines and in driving back and forth, we could be in the kitchen cooking "from scratch."

Yet many of us are developing a new consciousness about the foods we eat, an awareness rarely lost by the rural folk. We know our food becomes one with us. We know the way we acquire and use our food directly affects and reflects other facets of our unconscious and conscious lives.

If we are paying close attention to the foods we choose, nurture, cook, and eat, then we are likely to be more in tune with other phases of our lives. But if we are careless about what we eat, we are probably rushing through our daily lives and missing both pleasure and good health.

Good food helps keep us strong and clearheaded. Preparing good food helps us slow down and pay attention.

More and more people are doing something direct to acquire their daily fare. They are making yogurt or sprouting mung beans at home. They are baking bread and planting gardens. Fresh vegetables for the table are being eked out of miniplots between apartment houses, while in the suburbs gardens seem to be increasing in size and frequency. And many people have even begun to keep small livestock to help supplement their diets.

As inflation rises and shortages increase in our unwieldy and unstable society, we'll be better off if we once again begin to take care of our own needs.

The benefits of nitty gritty "home-done" foods are:

- Better health from the hours spent outdoors and from fresh food.
- Money saved.
- Gourmet flavors earned.
- Less waste and better recycling.
- Availability.
- Convenience of selecting garden-fresh food right before eating.
- Peace of mind knowing your food comes without plastics, pesticides, and preservatives.
- Closeness to nature and relaxation during busy daily lives.

Think of the joy that comes from a half hour spent among the plants and creatures large and small, while the sun is rising or setting and the air is crisp, the sky beautiful, and the earth seems at peace. Picking strawberries before the sun is high, rinsing them in a quiet cozy kitchen, and slicing them directly onto a bowl of fresh granola covered with creamy goat's milk. A breakfast

egg just gathered, and a slice of freshbaked whole-grain bread. Mint and rose hips gathered for tea in the woods on a pleasant walk the week before. The pottery bowl and the peacefulness—a far cry from the plastic snack grabbed in the crowded automat and hurriedly eaten from throwaway dishes with plastic "silverware."

Oh, yes, I hear you! You tell me you have to live in the city, and though you dream of living closer to nature you just can't—right now.

And I say—you *can* take a step closer. You can grow those strawberries and maybe some lettuce and a few other things in boxes on your tiny terrace. You can attach them to the outside wall in an attractive pattern. You can pick enough berries for the morning cereal while you watch the birds gather at your feeder. You can bake fresh bread. You may have to forego the fresh milk and eggs, but you can go one step closer with raw certified milk and organic eggs obtained from your nearest health food store. You can grow mushrooms and sprouts for lunch in your kitchen, too.

While you're enjoying better food, better health, and a quieter pace, you can tuck away the dollars you save for the time when you move to your one-acre plot in the suburbs or your isolated farm in the woods.

Or if you thrive on busy city life but wish to enrich it, these steps will make your life more pleasant and, likely, longer. But you must *start* today to live a little closer to the life style you visualize as ideal.

If you're already living on your acre or on your farm, I'll tell you how you can grow most of your own food with little effort and hassle. *Everything* mentioned in NITTY GRITTY FOODBOOK can be done on a one-acre plot, from vegetables and fruit to small livestock.

And while you're developing your self-sufficiency, you will be learning more about nature's cycle and your part in it. You will develop a consciousness for establishing your own mini-ecological cycle. You will compost your scraps in a plastic bag under the apartment sink to create a few pots of good soil for your minigarden. Or you'll have a vast compost heap complete with hundreds of worms somewhere between the house, the garden, and the barn. In either case, you'll grow more aware of the give and take in nature's pattern.

Here's my family's formula for nitty gritty living. We live on less than one acre of horizontal mountain land, terraced and surrounded by vertical land. We have a small garden, a large compost pile (full of worms), goats, chickens, dogs, and a cat. Our barn space is a meager 10 x 8 feet.

During the summer, the garden supplies almost all the family vegetables, with many preserved for winter use. The waste from the vegetables is fed to the chickens and goats, thus supplementing their feed. The extra milk is fed to the dogs, chickens, and cat. The cat, looking forward to his twice-daily ration of milk, lives in the little barn, protecting the livestock's grain from marauding rodents.

The dogs, being territorial creatures at heart, keep stray dogs and wild animals from killing the goats and chickens—and they get the extra milk and cracked eggs. Three dozen chickens supply more than enough eggs for our family and a few to sell to neighbors and friends. There are also enough eggs to trade for all the goats' hay. As the insects hatch in the spring, the chickens go wild searching for fresh bugs to supplement their diet, thus helping the garden and the aesthetics of our surroundings.

The goats eat the weeds and prunings that would take a long time to compost, or would otherwise be taken to the dump. And our favorite milk goat, Sukie, single-udderedly supplies three to four quarts of milk a day—plenty for our family of five for all the breakfast milk, cocoa, custards and puddings, ice cream and other goodies we want, plus some for guests and extra to keep the animals sleek. Most of our animals are gentle, tame, named, and a pleasure.

On our tiny plot of earth, several wild things grow which we use frequently—lamb's quarters for spring greens; sage to use sparingly as a fresh herb with plenty to gather for winter; mint of several varieties for cool iced tea and hot spiced tea; one variety of edible mushrooms to perk up spring vegetables; dandelions for salad, cooked greens, and wine; wild chokecherry for wine and jelly; plus several old-fashioned medicinal herbs and undoubtedly many plants whose use we are not aware of.

We recycle conscientiously. All organic wastes go on the compost pile or to the animals. Many of our fruits and vegetables are home-canned in the fall, so we reuse the jars from year to year and throw away few cans. We have no milk cartons to throw away; milk is kept in shiny, clear jars that are not suitable for home canning. Egg cartons are used over and over. We feel our family still contributes too much to the throwaway society, but we have improved.

Before you visualize a lush verdant forest as the site of our home, I must hasten to tell you we live in relatively dry, steep mountains at nearly 7,000 feet. Snow can fall nine months of the year, although it usually doesn't. July and August are likely to be hot and dry, with well and stream slowing to a trickle. It is beautiful but impractical. But gardening can still be done by mixing rich compost with the decomposed granite soil and by using mulch to conserve heat and moisture. Goats and chickens can grow fat on land that appears to nourish nothing but pines. In winter the sun shines often, though days are cold and crisp. And the animals' coats grow thick and warm.

Oh, yes, we do long for a gently rolling farm with woods and meadows, a babbling brook, four frost-free months, and substantial, picturesque buildings. We plan that, but continue to utilize and grow in the here and now, which is all any of us really have.

NUTRITION

If you are to remain healthy, your food must contain a balance of a wide variety of elements. "Balance" is the key word; there must be a balance of carbohydrates, fats, and proteins; minerals and vitamins; acid and alkaline substances. These must come from a variety of foods, the main groups of which are fruits and vegetables; grains and cereals; meats, poultry, fish, dairy products; and seeds, nuts, and oils. The balance is necessary because almost no food contains all elements, and elements work in groups, catalyzing and freeing one another to work.

Carbohydrates include sugars and starches. Their job is to provide short-term blood sugar and energy. Whole grains, fruits, and vegetables provide proper carbohydrates, while white sugar and white flour do not. Cellulose (fibrous materials) furnishes bulk in the diet.

Fats fall into two categories: vegetable fats such as corn oil, and animal fats such as lard. Their job is to provide long-term energy and tone the skin and muscles. They also make up part of the cell structure, cushion the organs, and supply an essential fatty acid, linoleic acid. Cold-pressed vegetable oils are best for general use; however, some animal fat is useful for the proper utilization of vitamin E. Fats carry vitamins A, D, E, and K and help the body use them.

Proteins are the cell builders. They also help make hemoglobin and antibodies and assist in supplying energy. Meat, fish, poultry, dairy products, eggs, nuts, beans, and lentils are foods high in proteins. However, you should choose from these foods as widely as possible, as proteins are made up of eighteen or more amino acids. Some your body can manufacture and some it cannot. Those it cannot make are called essential amino acids, and food that contains them all is called a complete protein. Only meat, fish, poultry, dairy products, and eggs are considered complete proteins, but sprouted grains and sprouted legumes are nearly so. In tests with animals, they alone have healthfully sustained life through several generations. Incomplete proteins may be combined in ways to create complete proteins, for example, beans with rice, soybeans with sesame seeds.

Considerably more effort is needed to repair sick bodies than to keep bodies healthy in the first place. Much more research needs to be done about the specific functions of vitamins and minerals in maintaining health. And certainly more study is needed about the interrelationship between physical health and emotional health. In any case, our bodies will function more efficiently if we eat properly.

Vitamin A is essential for growth, reproduction, and healthy body tissue with good tone. Shortages can cause skin problems, night blindness, susceptibility to infections, and glandular and organ difficulties. Vitamin A helps to stimulate growth, to build new cells, and to promote long life. The best sources are butter, cheese, cream, and milk (preferably raw milk from healthy animals), tomatoes and other fruits. Spinach, carrots, and other dark-green and deep-yellow vegetables contain carotene, which your body can change into vitamin A.

Vitamin B is really a complex of vitamins—thiamin, niacin, riboflavin, and others. The big job the B vitamins have is to help in releasing food energy, to prevent anemia, and to vitalize the nervous system, especially in times of stress. Nervous disorders may result from their shortage. The B vitamins are also important in maintaining healthy glands and organs. The best sources of the B vitamins are meats, whole grains, all leafy dark-green vegetables, liver and organ meats, dry beans and lentils, spinach, carrots, tomatoes, potatoes, cabbage, turnips, and brewer's yeast.

Vitamin C is needed to keep the blood vessels healthy, to prevent and fight infection, to help in cementing body cells together, and to assist in bone and tooth formation. Vitamin C is the one vitamin neither manufactured nor stored by the body and must be had daily. It is a natural detoxifying agent. It is fragile and destroyed by smoking and by the heat required for pasteurization. Shortages can cause difficulties with the gums, loose teeth, long-lasting bruises, and a susceptibility to infectious disease. Vitamin C is a vitalizer and energizer. The best sources of vitamin C are citrus fruits, tomatoes, cabbage, green beans, carrots, sprouting grains, dark leafy vegetables, wild edible green plants, rose hips, pine and spruce needles, green peppers, and raw milk.

Vitamin D is necessary for strong bones and teeth. Shortages may result in bone difficulties or possibly in nervousness or restlessness. Best sources of vitamin D are raw milk, coconut, fish and fish oils, egg yolk, spinach, swiss chard, dandelions, and sunlight. Sunlight is needed for the body to manufacture vitamin D.

Vitamin E is considered to be the energy vitamin. It aids in vitality, reproduction, strength, and assists in maintaining youthful body tissues. Foods rich in vitamin E are wheat germ, red meats, green leaves, cold-pressed vegetable oils, and butterfat.

The body requires many minerals. Some are:

Calcium. Responsible for hardness of teeth and bones and proper functioning of body tissues and fluids. Found in dairy products, salmon, soybeans, and dark-green leafy vegetables.

Iodine. Necessary to proper functioning of the thyroid gland. Found in iodized salt, seafood, and sea salt.

Iron. Combines with protein to make hemoglobin, which carries oxygen to cells. Found in organ meats, dry beans and peas, dark-green vegetables, egg yolk, and molasses.

Magnesium and phosphorus. Help in body's use of food for energy. Found in nuts, whole grains, dry beans and peas, and dark-green leafy vegetables. Phosphorus is generally found in the same foods that provide protein and calcium.

In addition, there are several trace minerals found primarily in a variety of vegetables. Wild edible plants seem especially high in necessary minerals.

Foods generally can be classed as acid- or alkaline-forming substances. To maintain proper health, it is thought the body needs a slightly alkaline pH, so somewhat more than half the foods you eat should be from the alkaline category.

Alkaline-forming foods include most vegetables, fruits, milk and yogurt, honey, and red wines.

Acid-forming foods include meat, fish, poultry, nuts, grains, cereals, pastas, soybeans, bread, cheese, butter, legumes, peas and lentils, brussel sprouts, asparagus, corn, and beer.

A balanced, varied diet will provide most essential vitamins and minerals. However, refined foods and depleted soil have had nutrients stolen from them (see chart below). It's best if you grow all the food you can as organically as possible, or obtain fresh, organic food from a reliable source.

Brown Rice Compared to White Rice

	Brown Rice	White Rice
Vitamins*		
Thiamin	0.34 mg.	0.07 mg.
Riboflavin	0.05 mg.	0.03 mg.
Niacin	4.7 mg.	1.6 mg.
Minerals*		
Calcium	32 mg.	24 mg.
Phosphorus	221 mg.	94 mg.
Iron	1.6 mg.	0.8 mg.
Potassium	214 mg.	92 mg.
Sodium	9 mg.	5 mg.
Protein*	7.5 g.	6.7 g.

Per 100 grams or 3-1/2 ounces.

SOURCE: "Composition of Foods," Agriculture Handbook, No. 8, *U.S. Department of Agriculture.*

A Daily Food Guide

*SERVINGS
RECOMMENDED*

A TYPICAL SERVING

Meat group

2 to 3 ounces of lean cooked meat, poultry, or fish. As alternates ... 1 egg, 1/2 cup cooked dry beans or peas, or 2 tablespoons of peanut butter may replace 1/2 serving of meat.

Milk group

One 8-ounce cup of fluid milk — whole,
Child, under 9 ..... *2 to 3* skim, buttermilk — or evaporated, or dry
Child, 9 to 12 . *3 or more* milk, reconstituted. As alternates ... 1-inch
Teenager ...... *4 or more* cube Cheddar-type cheese, 2/3 cup cottage
Adult .... *2 or more* cheese or ice milk, or 1 cup ice cream may
Pregnant woman *3 or more* replace 1/2 cup of fluid milk.
Nursing woman. *4 or more*

Vegetable-fruit group
4 or more, including:

1/2 cup of vegetable or fruit; or a portion, for example, 1 medium apple, banana, or potato, half a medium grapefruit or cantaloupe.

*One important source of vita-
min C*

Important sources:
Grapefruit, orange, lemon, and tangerine (fruit or juice); cantaloupe; guava; honeydew melon; mango; papaya; raw strawberries; watermelon. Asparagus tips; broccoli; brussels sprouts; raw cabbage; collards; green or sweet red peppers; kale; kohlrabi; mustard greens; potatoes and sweet potatoes cooked in jacket; spinach; tomatoes or their juice; turnip greens.

*One important source of vita-
min A—at least every other
day*

Important sources:
Dark-green and deep-yellow vegetables and a few fruits, namely: apricots; broccoli; cantaloupe; carrots; Swiss chard; collards; watercress; kale; mango; persimmon; pumpkin; spinach; sweet potatoes; turnip greens, and other dark-green leaves; winter squash.

Bread-cereal group
4 or more

Count only if whole-grain or enriched:
1 slice of bread or similar serving of baked goods made with whole-grain or enriched flour, 1 ounce ready-to-eat cereal, 1/2 to 3/4 cup cooked cereal, cornmeal, grits, spaghetti, macaroni, noodles, or rice.

SOURCE: "Your Money's Worth in Foods," Home and Gardening Bulletin, No. 183, *U.S. Department of Agriculture.*

FOOD FACILITIES

If you are becoming a nitty gritty cook, you will need as usable a kitchen as possible. You will need space to work and lots of storage. You will want to create a pleasant environment to enjoy.

Your kitchen should have plenty of shelves to hold the jams and pickles, the fruits and vegetables you'll can. Shelves and cupboards for storing fruits and vegetables can be located anywhere. You'll need a large space to store preserving equipment—your canner and pressure canner, ricer and blancher, and all those empty jars soon to be filled with goodies.

I personally favor the return of the pantry, long omitted from the modern kitchen. A pantry is a little room located off the kitchen with broad shelves reaching from floor to ceiling, with hooks for hanging, and with all the space necessary to put everything needed in a kitchen. The pantry is very handy, particularly for items that are bulky or that are used infrequently. Canned goods will keep better in a pantry, too, as there is less heat and light.

For cold storage, your kitchen, garage, or basement should have space for a large freezer. Ideally, you should also have a cool storage room in the basement, or a cellar outside in which to store your root vegetables. It should keep a constant temperature of 35° to 45° year round, be watertight, yet have a little constant humidity and ventilation. Potatoes, onions, carrots, squashes, pumpkins and other vegetables won't need to be canned or frozen if stored in a proper cellar or basement.

You also need a place to store grains and other staples that you keep in quantity, a place both moistureproof and creatureproof. One workable solution for storing such staples is large, sturdy trash cans with tight lids. You might use large, plastic yard bags, but they alone are not sturdy or mouseproof, and mice may gossip and travel a long distance to search out your goodies.

Kitchenware and appliances can be most easily and inexpensively located through one of the large mail-order catalogs like Ward's or Sears', who also offer good guarantees.

In choosing pots and pans, I suggest stainless steel, ceramic, and cast iron. These pans offer great durability, good heat distribution, easy washing, and no exchange of impurities from the pan to the food. They also remain attractive.

For frying, nothing can compare with cast iron. After using it, wipe out your cast-iron frying pan with a cloth coated with cooking oil rather than washing it. This will keep the pan "seasoned" and maintain the cooking quality. If it doesn't wipe clean, wash and scour it, then re-oil, or the food will stick next time.

For very large pots, cast iron is usually impractical because of its weight. Ceramic works well, but is more expensive and usually not available in large sizes; also, I have broken it. Stainless steel lasts many years and is available in quite large sizes. I recommend it for everything but frying.

A Chinese wok comes in handy for stir-frying vegetables, a method that maintains color, flavor, and nutritional value.

A pressure cooker is almost essential for saving time and nutrients. It is one key to cooking meals from "scratch" quickly. It can cook almost anything in less than an hour, including dry beans. Most foods are cooked within a few minutes. Buy a stainless steel model if you can afford it. Otherwise settle for the heavy cast-aluminum variety, but remove food from the cooker immediately after cooking is complete.

Some people are afraid of pressure cookers, but there is no need to be, if you follow the simple directions. My mother once had a pressure cooker blow a potful of beef and noodles through the tiny hole in the lid. The greasy food hung everywhere, from ceiling and walls, counters and windows. She'd gone to take a bath and left the heat on high. You can't do that. We cleaned and laughed for a long time.

I find the pressure cookers made during the 1950's to be more substantial than the new models, whose handles fall off and whose metal is thinner. Used pressure cookers can be found at Goodwill, the Salvation Army, and rummage sales. Do not buy one that is pitted or bent in any way. Before shopping, make yourself familiar enough with general pressure-cooker construction to be sure all parts are there. A used model will probably need a new rubber ring and possibly a new pressure gauge. They are obtainable at good hardware stores or through mail-order catalogs.

When selecting kitchen appliances, you must consider the number of people to be served, the fuel source, the price, and your own preference. If you have a community-type kitchen and cook in large quantities, you might have to visit a restaurant supply house or an army surplus store to find the size utensils you need. You should also have a copy of *Quantity Recipes,* published by the Cornell Home Economics Extension. (See *Suggested Reading.*)

There are a large number of small electrical appliances available for every conceivable purpose. A blender is one of the few I feel is justified. It is a good practical tool and a proper use of electricity. An electric mixer and a toaster are probably justified and worthwhile, but most other gadgets are both a waste of money and a waste of power. The disposal is one of the worst—it cheats both soil and animals of food potential. Carefully consider your real needs before acquiring a kitchen full of gadgets that use valuable energy.

Dishwashers are a great help in reducing family tension and drudgery over dirty dishes. They aid in preventing the spread of colds and other infections. They do use excessive electricity, but you can omit the drying cycle, which uses the most. They also use a little more water, but not much more than a careless human. Dishwashers are great for washing and sterilizing the dozens of canning jars needed during the summer and fall.

For cold storage, you need a refrigerator and probably a freezer. A large refrigerator-freezer may be sufficient for a small family.

For more people, you'll need a large refrigerator and a large freezer. For storing quantities of frozen food on a slim budget, rent a large food locker. Costs are little, depending on the size, and often less than the cost of electricity to run a freezer at home. The food locker provides storage for foods bought when prices are low. Bring home a few packages at a time as you need them and keep them in your refrigerator-freezer.

Used refrigerators and freezers are generally a good buy—usually they either work or they don't work at all. For storing very large quantities, and especially if you hunt or produce your own meat, you may want to build an entire refrigerated room. Do so cheaply by obtaining the refrigeration unit from an old grocery store.

For refrigeration in homes without electricity, you can rely on old gas refrigerators found at auctions or secondhand stores. They seem to run on and on.

In selecting a kitchen range, you'll choose from many sizes and kinds. I think a wide oven is imperative, but most other details can be left to individual taste.

Fuel sources available are electricity, propane or natural gas, wood, or coal. I prefer gas because it responds instantly, is inexpensive, and is less subject to power outages. Electricity is cleaner in the kitchen. For remote areas, a combination propane gas, coal, and wood stove is an excellent compromise. Fine gas and electric ranges are inexpensive on the secondhand market.

The Wood Cookstove

The wood cookstove is a marvelous invention and a real necessity in locations without ready access to electricity and heating gas. It provides both heat for cooking and room heat—a boon in winter, a bane in summer. A good wood stove will do the job of a gas or electric stove. Skilled cooks claim wood cookstoves bake much better.

More people today are building their cabin in the woods and using a coal and wood stove for the first time. It can be painful to be faced with that hulk of a stove that doesn't have a single push button. Below is an old-style wood cookstove, a luxury, top-of-the-line model. So that your learning will be smooth, here's how to use it.

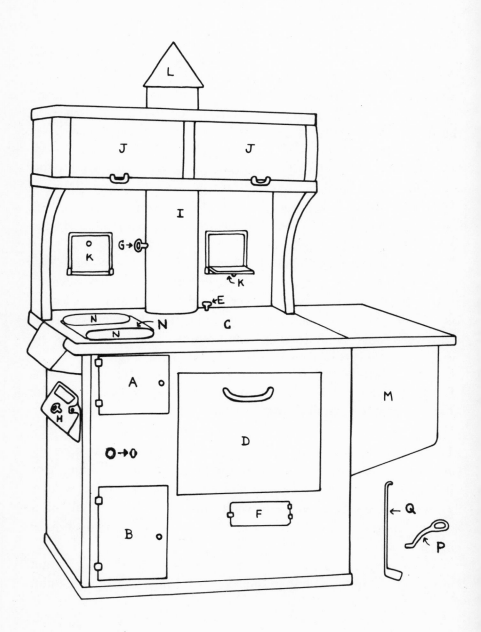

WOOD COOKSTOVE OPERATION

A. Firebox. Here the fire is started and fed.

B. Ashbox. Container for ashes and their removal.

C. Stove Top. A flat cast-iron cooking surface.

D. Oven. For baking; looks and cooks the same as a modern oven.

E. Oven Damper. A shut-off valve for the stove pipe; controls oven heat.

F. Oven Clean-Out. Collects ashes that accumulate in smoke passages that heat oven.

G. Stove Pipe Damper. Controls the amount of smoke going up the pipe.

H. Firebox Damper. Controls rate of combustion within the firebox.

I. Stove Pipe. Carries smoke out of stove and kitchen. Must be at least four feet higher than roof.

J. Warming Ovens. Keep cooked food warm.

K. Flip Down Warmers. For keeping coffee pots and tea kettles warm.

L. Stove Pipe Cap. Keeps rain and wind out of stove pipe.

M. Water Reservoir. Heats water for washing while stove cooks.

N. Burner and Centerpiece. Removable for feeding fire and for direct-heat cooking.

O. Ash Grate Bolt. Turns to dump ashes from grates into ashbox.

P. Lid Remover. For lifting burner lids, opening oven doors, pushing dampers, turning ash grate bolt.

Q. Oven Hoe. For removing ashes.

For some time my friend Suzy Braithwaite has used only a wood cookstove. I pass on many of her suggestions.

To start and maintain a fire

1. Open all dampers wide. **(E)**, **(G)**, **(H)**.

2. Clean out ashes from firebox **(A)**. Turn ash grate bolt (**O**) causing grates to shift and dump ashes into ashbox **(B)**, using end of the lid remover **(P)**. Clean out every time a fire is lighted.

3. Check the ash box **(B)**. If it is nearly full, dump it. CAUTION:

Treat all ashes as if they were hot. Dump them into a covered metal bucket or covered hole outside. Many a cabin fire has been caused by "cool" ashes in a bucket burning through the floor overnight.

4. Check the oven clean-out (F) and perhaps peek under the top of the range plate to see how much ash has accumulated. If necessary, clean these areas with the oven hoe (Q). The oven won't heat if smoke passages around it are clogged with ashes.

5. Remove the two burner lids (N) and centerpiece (N) with lid remover (P) so top of the firebox is open.

Build a fire in the following way:

6. Insert crushed newspaper, about three lengthwise rolls.

7. On top of that place very thin pieces of wood or twigs diagonally the length of the firebox, then a second layer on the diagonal, crossing the first. The third layer of wood can be thicker than the first two. Use about four layers total.

8. Replace the centerpiece first, then the burner lids.

9. Through the door of the firebox, light a match to the paper. Close the firebox door to contain and spread the flames.

10. When the burning wood drops, add more, also placed on the diagonal. This allows space to improve the oxygen flow for maximum efficiency. The initial fire is a hot one. To make even more heat, add larger pieces of wood.

To cook

Start a fire with all dampers wide open. This allows as much air to flow in as possible. Once the fire is established, carefully close the stove pipe damper (G) part way to slow down the passage of the hot smoke out the chimney, thus keeping the heat in the stove. If smoke begins to seep from around the burners, you have closed the damper too much.

Close the oven damper (E) to channel more heat to the oven, or leave oven damper open for burner heat. The oven temperature can be lowered by opening the oven damper and closing other dampers. To lower temperature of oven further, open oven clean-out door and possibly oven door.

Your fire should now be burning well on small to medium-size pieces of wood. Put in large chunks of wood to maintain heat. Also close the firebox damper to slow down combustion. This is called "banking the fire" and it keeps the fire going with a minimum amount of wood.

When cooking on a wood stove, you use a combination of all three dampers to get the amount of heat you want with the least waste of wood.

Hints

● Greasy paper helps in starting a fire, as does wood containing pitch.

● Very tiny wood chips make excellent kindling for starting the fire.

● Firewood is anything that will burn—green wood, dry wood, old boards. Each has its merits. Dry wood is preferred as it catches easily and burns fast. Cedar is hotter than pine, oak hotter than cedar, and maple hottest of all. The harder the wood, the hotter the fire. Green wood will keep a fire going for a long time without additional wood. However, it will cause smoking, unless there's a fairly hot fire going when the green wood is added. Green wood helps in slow baking. Get to know the available woods. Learn to select the best wood to provide the kind of fire you need.

● By removing a burner, you can set a pan directly over the flames, if desired. Chappatis or tortillas may be browned directly on the range top.

● Get to know your stove intimately. A wood stove, like a temperamental artist, requires a lot of tending and attention. Learn where its hot spots and cool spots are. Learn how to shift pots cooking on the stove top to get the right amount of heat. The farther from the firebox, the cooler the stove will be.

● Even if the oven has a thermometer on the door, it is wise to add a thermometer inside for accurate temperatures.

● When setting up a wood stove, make sure it's level. This is important.

Selecting a wood cookstove

A wood cookstove may be somewhat difficult to find. Many sit as planters in plush family rooms, or rust in backyards. Prices can be high because of their desirability as antiques, although some modern wood stoves are being made. Check secondhand stores, antique stores, and auctions in rural areas, or run a classified ad.

In selecting a wood stove, first check inside the firebox. The linings should be in one piece with no holes; grates should not be broken; the cast-iron walls of the stove should not be broken or warped. It is very difficult to obtain replacement parts.

Decide on the best size for your needs. Smaller stoves are easier to move and take less space. The fancier models have conveniences like warming ovens and water reservoirs. A good supply of hot water provided by a water reservoir can be a real convenience if you don't have hot running water.

A gas hot plate supplied by a small propane bottle is a convenient supplement to the wood cookstove during hot summer months. Be sure neither the hot plate nor the gas line is near the hot cookstove. In summer, a pressure cooker also helps speed wood cookstove cookery.

Coal cookstoves offer the advantage of more lasting, sustained heat. Many cookstoves are interchangeable for coal and wood. The difference between the coal cookstove and the wood cookstove is in the firebox. The firebox of a wood cookstove will be longer, to accommodate sticks of wood.

Knife Sharpening

Many kitchens lack a sharp knife and many cooks lack knife-sharpening skills.

Buy a double-grit flat sharpening stone, fine on one side and medium on the other. Oil the stone with household oil before sharpening your knife. This keeps the metal shavings from working down into the stone. Hold the knife blade at a 35° angle to the stone, and move the blade in a circular motion, first against the medium stone, then the fine. (If your knife is sharp and you simply want to hone the edge, use the fine grit only.) Turn the knife over in your hand and sharpen it against the stone at the same angle, with the same circular motion; however, now you're sharpening the opposite side of the blade. Take off the feather edge by stropping on a piece of leather tightly secured at both ends, blade against the strop, sweeping first away from you on one side of the knife blade, then sweeping toward you with the other side of the knife blade.

This is only one of the many ways that folks sharpen their knives. However, Tim Herdt, who has lots of experience with knives, likes this way best.

I can recommend both Old Hickory and Sabatier knives. Keep your knife away from heat and flame so the temper of the blade will not be damaged. Keep it clean and dry, and it will serve you for many years.

WHERE TO GET FOOD

Foods are obtained from three main sources. They can be purchased, grown, or foraged. Purchasing requires lots of money, little time, little work, some know-how. Growing requires a little money, some time, lots of work, some know-how. Foraging requires no money, lots of time, some work, lots of know-how. You'll have to decide which combination best suits your needs.

Purchasing

Following are basic items for stocking your nitty gritty cupboard—ingredients that will tide you through most recipes and most emergencies. These staples have good keeping qualities. They are easily bought in quantity monthly or less frequently. Starred items (*) can also be easily made in your kitchen or raised on your acre, as described in this book.

Salt
Baking powder
Baking soda
Flour* (unbleached, wheat, rye)
Yeast (refrigerate)
Honey*
Dry powdered milk
Tea (regular and herb)

Curry powder
Cinnamon
Other favorite spices and herbs
Nuts (raw cashews, almonds, walnuts)
Carob powder
Cocoa powder
Rice (brown)

Coffee

Oregano

Black pepper

Spaghetti* (preferably high
protein)

Wheat germ (refrigerate)

Chili pepper

Barley

Dry split peas

Dry white or pinto beans*

Macaroni* (preferably
whole wheat)

Unsaturated cooking oil

Canned goods*

The following staples you can buy more frequently, perhaps monthly or semimonthly. However, with the proper cold-storage area, they can be kept for months.

Onions *

Potatoes *

Carrots *

Cabbage *

Squash *

Frozen foods *

Following are items you must buy weekly or semimonthly.

Milk *

Eggs *

Cheese *

Meat, fish, and poultry *

Fresh vegetables *

Fresh fruits *

Butter *

Food varies in price according to the quantity you are able to purchase and where and when you purchase it.

The larger the quantity you are able to buy, the cheaper your food will cost per unit. Therefore, always have in mind the intended use for the food and the time it will be stored.

Buy fruits and vegetables around harvest time, then can, freeze, and preserve enough for the months ahead. After you learn the techniques, the time expenditure is not great. You will have a good supply on hand at a cheap price, and it will not be necessary to run to the grocery store every evening before fixing dinner.

Most foods have a season when they are abundant and cheaper, be they fresh, canned, or frozen. So if your space allows, stock up at that prime time. The butcher and the produce manager at your supermarket will advise you if you don't have direct access to the grower.

If you live in a one-room apartment, quantity savings may not be possible, but you can still try to buy the in-season food each week—and notice some savings. Also, you can save by joining or organizing a food co-op.

Foraging

Not so many years ago supermarkets did not exist. How then did humans eat? How did they supplement cultivated foods, and how did mankind eat before food plants were cultivated? Foods were foraged, gathered from the forests and the meadows.

Today foods may still be foraged, if you will but take the time. Foraging foods is soul-satisfying; many foraged foods are delicious and satisfy the body in a delightful fashion. Foraged foods offer the advantages of greater hardiness and, generally speaking, several times the nutritional value of domestic cultivated food plants of similar varieties.

Below are listed common foods to forage—from the vacant lot, the field, the city park, the wilderness. No matter where you live, whether urban or rural, these foods are likely to be available to you, as they grow coast to coast.

Wild plants are used today as food plants in most parts of the world. Yet in our society, most of them are considered weeds. "Weeds" simply means that they grow hardily where they are not intended by man. However, since modern man, in his fervent effort to force nature to comply with his wishes, seeks to eradicate these weeds, one must be careful not to gather wild foods where they might be sprayed with weed killer. It seems ironic to me that we often struggle to destroy the bountiful edible food plants in our gardens, then struggle again to force some puny hybrid import to feed us well.

When gathering wild edible plants, carefully clip the plant above the ground so that it may grow again to nourish some creature. Most of these plants are available for gathering from the first frost to the last. Some flourish before the first frost and after the last frost. However, to be used as greens, the tender, young, spring leaves are best.

DANDELIONS

Dandelions hardly need identification; if by some quirk of fate you've never known them, any suburbanite should be able to point them out in his lawn. Every bit of the dandelion has use as food, food in abundance and variety.

• *Salad.* Wash **young, tender leaves.** Toss in **olive oil** and **lemon juice.** Garnish with **chopped chives, parsley, garlic,** and **bacon bits.**

• *Coffee.* Roast the clean **roots** in a 250⁰ oven about 4 hours, until they brown and pop. Store in a covered jar until needed. Then grind and brew as with regular coffee, using less. Tastes similar to coffee.

• *Flower wine.* Follow recipe in *Frivolities* (page 124.)

• *Root vegetable.* Use like parsnips or salsify. Peel the **roots** with a potato peeler, then slice crosswise. Simmer in **two waters.** In **the first water** with **a pinch of soda,** simmer until you can stick them with a fork. Then drain and simmer in **fresh water** until tender and they break apart easily with a fork. Drain and season with **salt, pepper,** and **butter.**

• *Crown salad.* Remove the **white crown** from the top of the roots. Soak in **cold salt water** until ready for use. Then eat raw in salads.

• *Steamed crowns.* Remove the **white crown** from the top of the root. Soak in **cold salt water** until ready for use. Then steam until tender and serve with **salt, pepper,** and **butter.**

● *Fried crowns*. Add **a half cup sautéed dandelion crowns** to your next **omelette**. Good with mushrooms.

● *Wilted crown salad*. Fry and drain **several slices of bacon**, reserving the fat. Add **2 tablespoons apple-cider vinegar** to the **bacon fat**. Sauté **crowns** in the fat and drain. Garnish with **bacon bits** and **hard-boiled egg**.

● *Steamed greens*. Gently steam **young, washed greens** until they become limp. Season with **salt** and **pepper, butter,** or **bacon.**

● *Steamed baby blossoms*. In early spring, before they bloom, remove the embryonic **blossoms** from beneath ground level. Wash and slice. Cover with **boiling water,** simmer 3 minutes, and drain. Season with **butter** and **salt.**

It's a shame dandelions are destroyed with weed killer, isn't it? Most people spend many hours each summer to dig them up and toss them in the alley; then they change clothes, rush off to the supermarket for fresh summer greens at 29¢ a pound or more, rush home to cook, and end up bringing a vegetable to the table containing much less nutritional value. Dandelions contain three times more iron than any other similar vegetables, plus valuable trace minerals.

PURSLANE

This annual hugs the ground, seldom growing more than 2 inches high, but often more than a foot across. Purslane is a common garden weed. Its tendrils are about 1/4 inch thick where they emerge from the center of the plant. At each forking of the stem, a tiny yellow flower blooms on sunny mornings. Purslane is gathered by pinching off the tender leafy tips. It is good raw, cooked, or pickled.

- *Soup.* **Tips** are delicious added to **split-pea soup.** Also, use in place of okra in **gumbo-style soups.**
- *Greens.* Wash, slice, and simmer **stems** 10 minutes. Season with **salt, pepper,** and **butter.**
- *Vegetable.* Wash, slice, and sauté in **bacon fat** 7 minutes. Season with **salt** and **vinegar.**
- *Casserole.* Simmer **tips** until tender. Stir in **one egg** and **bread crumbs** until mixture is thick. Bake in a casserole at 350° until brown. Serve.
- *Pickles.* Substitute **stems** for cucumbers in any pickle recipe. A delicious addition to the dill crock.
- *Flour.* Dry **whole plants** on a sheet. Thresh to remove seeds. Shake through strainer to remove any particles, and grind the **seeds** into flour. Use half and half with **whole-wheat flour** to make delicious buckwheat pancakes or muffins.

DAY LILIES

These tall, wild lilies with their large, orange blossoms speckled with brown are frequently found in yards and wild places. They can be used in salads and stews, and the blossoms provide one of the best flowers for eating.

- *Stew.* Gather **wilted or fresh day lily blossoms.** Spread them to dry, then store in a jar. Add to **soup or stew** during the last 15 minutes of cooking.
- *Vegetable.* Simmer **day lily buds** as you would green beans. Season with **butter, salt,** and **pepper.**
- *Fried flowers.* Dip **buds or blossoms** in an **egg-and-flour batter,** then fry until golden brown.
- *Tubers.* Remove the tender young **tubers** from day lily roots any time the ground is not frozen. Set the root back in the earth after removing these tubers and it will continue to grow. Use the tubers steamed, creamed, or raw in salads.
- *Stalks.* Use the new **stalks** that sprout in the spring. Cut them off just above the root. Steam like asparagus or serve raw in tossed salad.
- *Day Lily gelatin mold.* Lay **blossoms** face down in molds. Fill molds with **clear or tinted liquid gelatin,** prepared according to the package directions. Refrigerate to firm. Unmold by running hot water over molds. Delightful, startling, and refreshing.

DAY LILY BLOSSOMS ORIENTAL

Cut **1/2 pound pork** into bite-size pieces and brown. Add **1 quart water, 2 tablespoons soy sauce,** and **1 teaspoon salt.** Simmer 1 hour, adding water if necessary. Add **1 firmly packed cup day lily blooms.** Cook until tender and serve hot.

SUNFLOWERS

The common wild sunflower provides seeds to be gathered for their high protein and fat content.

● *Sunflower seeds.* Gather the **flower heads,** dry and thresh them to remove seeds. Set a food chopper on a coarse setting and put the **seeds,** unhulled, through the chopper. Then stir the seeds in **water**; the hulls will float and the seeds will sink. Drain. Spread the seeds on a cookie sheet and roast them at 350° for at least 20 minutes. The longer you roast them, the sweeter they become. **Salt** if desired. Use the seeds as a snack or as a substitute for nuts in any recipe.

● *Sunflower seed meal.* Grind **sunflower seeds** through your finest food chopper blade. Add sunflower seed meal to any bread, cookie, or cake recipe. Make a delicious bread or cracker spread by mixing the **marrow from a cooked beef bone** with the sunflower meal. Very healthful.

WILD ROSES

Rose hips are the red-to-orange seed pods left on the wild rose bush after the flower petals fall. They may be gathered in the autumn and dried for use throughout the year. Rose hips contain more vitamin C than orange juice does. Remember, cooking at high temperatures will destroy vitamin C. The petals, of course, must be gathered in the summer.

• *Rose hip tea.* Simmer the **rose hips, crushed or whole,** to make a delicious tea. Ready when the tea becomes deep in color, about 12 minutes.

• *Rose hip jam.* Cut stem and blossom off **rose hips.** Slit and remove seeds. Blend together **1 cup hips** and the **juice of 1 lemon.** Add **3/4 cup warm honey,** stirring and blending well. Refrigerate. Use as a spread for pancakes and bread.

• *Rose hip soup.* This light soup is both fragrant and delicious. Simmer **2 cups rose hips** in **1 quart of water** for about 12 minutes. Sieve the hips to remove the seeds and skins. Add **water** to make 1 quart. Then add **1/2 cup sugar** and heat. Mix **1 tablespoon cornstarch** into a paste with **a little cold water.** Stir into soup mixture and cook a few minutes. Garnish with **a teaspoon of yogurt.**

• *Rose petal honey.* Add **1 cup washed rose petals** to **2 cups honey.** Bring to a boil and remove from heat. Let sit 6 hours. Bring to boil again, remove from heat and strain. Keep honey tightly closed.

ROSE PETAL OMELETTE

Blend:
8 eggs
1 teaspoon celery salt
Dash marjoram
1/2 cup clean rose petals

Pour into a hot, greased cast-iron skillet and cover. Cook until firm on top, brown on bottom, then fold in half. Garnish with **rose petals and buds.**

The food value of wild edible plants often exceeds the food value of domestic cultivated plants. For example, dandelion greens have almost twice the vitamin A of spinach. Lamb's quarters have almost twice the vitamin C of spinach, and spinach is one of our most nutritious garden vegetables. Purslane has 1-1/2 times the vitamin A of leaf lettuce and 8 times the vitamin A of iceberg lettuce. Purslane has 1-1/2 times the vitamin C of leaf lettuce and 3 times that of iceberg lettuce. Wild rose hips contain many times more vitamin C than an equal weight of oranges. Hulled sunflower seeds have several times the protein of sirloin of beef and a much greater mineral content. Protein and mineral content is also generally higher for wild edible plants than for garden vegetables.*

I offer the above information just as an introduction to the abundant storehouse of wild food plants nature has waiting to serve your palate and your purse. This is only a beginning, only the most common of the commonly available wild foods. I hope you will be intrigued enough to develop your own knowledge of foraging that which is so freely provided.

*Vegetable nutritional values are from Euell Gibbons, *Stalking the Healthful Herbs* (David McKay Company, 1973), pp. 271, 275-76.

I am indebted to Euell Gibbons for his books and delicious suggestions for using wild foods. I highly recommend his books to you. (See *Suggested Reading*.) They have helped reinforce and develop the bits and pieces of foraging knowledge which I have accumulated over the years.

The knowledge of foraging is as old as mankind, but like much old knowledge, it is nearly lost to our century, at least in Western society. We must keep it alive, for it may be needed again one day. And foraging is so fulfilling in the here and now.

You might as well take some paper bags along on your next hike and forage something for dinner.

HOW TO PROCESS
YOUR OWN FOOD

Fresh Dairy Foods

MILK

If you are able to keep a dairy animal, the milk you will have will be of an entirely different quality than that you purchase. In fact, my family dislikes drinking purchased fresh milk while the goats are dry—they claim it tastes too bad. At best, what you buy as "whole milk" is watery by comparison. If you live in a city, you may wish to try raw certified milk from a grocer or health-food store.

Since your own homestead milk is raw rather than pasteurized, you are assured of a more nutritionally sound food. Fresh, unpasteurized milk contains many B vitamins, and also A, C, and D, plus enzymes beneficial to your digestive system in general and specifically to the digestion of milk. Some of these nutritional benefits are lost in the heating required in pasteurization.

Of course, you must be sure that your animals are in the best health if you are to forego pasteurization, as that process was intended to destroy organisms that transmit disease from animal to man.

In caring for fresh milk, cleanliness is essential. It is necessary to strain the milk to remove small foreign particles. I have found that it helps also to milk through a strainer. This method keeps foreign matter from ever touching the milk. Then, before

refrigerating, pour that milk through a milk filter or coffee filter to remove any tiny particles of dust or dirt that were not caught in the strainer.

Milk is pasteurized by heating at 161^0 for 15 seconds, or at 142^0 for 30 minutes. This is best done in a double boiler or by heating the milk in a jar set in a pan of water. Avoid higher temperatures, as the boiling of milk changes both the taste and the nutritional value.

It is most important that milk be cooled to 50^0 or less as quickly as possible after milking to prevent excessive proliferation of bacteria, which causes souring and other chemical changes.

The containers used for milking and the storing of milk should be as germ-free as possible. This should be done either by boiling to sterilize, or by adding a few drops of chlorine bleach to the hot washing water. After rinsing, let the items air-dry. A dishwasher set on "sani-wash" will do a good job.

CREAM

If your milk comes from cows, the cream will separate from the milk, rising to the top of the container after setting in the refrigerator for a while. If you keep goats, the cream separates very slowly; generally it must be separated from the milk by a mechanical separator. Goat's milk is naturally homogenized. Homogeneity refers to the blending of the fat globules uniformly throughout the milk.

Preserving milk and cream

When you have extra milk and cream during the spring and summer, or when the animal is fresh, you may want to preserve some for later, when the animal is dry.

Milk and cream may be frozen. They will break down more slowly if pasteurized first. Cream may be frozen in ice-cube trays. Package the cubes in moistureproof wrap and store in your freezer. Then thaw for small serving portions. Milk may be frozen in well-washed 46-ounce juice cans. Those with replaceable pop-tops are especially good. Just leave an inch of head room for the expansion caused by freezing. Frozen milk and cream will keep four to six months at 0°F.

Of course, the oldest and best way to preserve milk for a long period is by cheesemaking, which is explained later in this chapter. There is no need to worry about spoilage—as cheese ages, the quality and flavor improve.

Before refrigeration, milk was kept fresh on the homestead by storing it in the cold cellar or in a springhouse with running, cool water. Extra cream was made into butter and kept in brine.

BUTTER

Cream is used to make butter. If you have no dairy animal, you can make butter from purchased heavy cream; however, there is generally no saving in this. A pint of heavy cream makes approximately a half pound of butter.

Have the heavy cream ready at about 58°. You can churn the butter either in an electric mixer at medium speed, in a hand-operated butter churn, or—patiently—by shaking in a quart jar.

Rinse your clean buttermaking implement with cold water right before using. Churn until the fat globules are the size of wheat grains or popcorn. Pour off the buttermilk to drink or to use in breadmaking. (It needs to be cultured to acquire the familiar sour buttermilk taste.)

Pour in water of about the same temperature and twice the quantity of the buttermilk. Churn it about four times. Wash the butter again. It's important to wash the butter thoroughly to take out all the buttermilk, or the butter will become rancid much more quickly. Work out all the water with your hands or a butter paddle, and work in salt if desired.

If you like flavored butter, you might work in some onion or garlic oil. Add butter coloring if you wish. This can be obtained from a dairy supply house. (In former times, marigolds were used to color butter.) Shape the butter, place in a dish, and cool.

Churning takes about 15 minutes with an electric mixer; about 20 to 30 minutes with a hand churn; and much longer by shaking in a jar. The time will vary according to the particular cream (the same animal's cream will vary from day to day), the temperature of the cream and the container, and even the weather. If it won't churn in a reasonable amount of time, check the temperature, let the cream set at room temperature for a couple of hours, and try again.

Obtaining an electric mixer, electric butter churn, or jar for churning isn't difficult. (Sears' and Ward's both offer an electric churn.) However, obtaining a hand churn is another story. I don't know a source for new hand churns. If you locate a source, please write me. Used hand churns can be located by determined sifting through rummage sales and secondhand stores. Many churns are considered to be antiques and can be found in fancy kitchens and recreation rooms serving as planters. You can find them in antique stores at quite ridiculous prices, but they are lovely.

One day the bright idea might strike that you can make butter in a blender. Ignore it—it only works in blenders with a quick, controlled cycle. Most blenders will only cut up the lumps of butter as they begin to form.

The butter that you make will be of a different color and texture than the butter you are accustomed to buying. Grocery butter almost always has added color and chemicals. Your cow's butter will be pale yellow; goat's butter will be almost white. Add butter coloring if you desire, but be aware that you're only satisfying your conditioning to bright-yellow commercial butter. The coloring you add must have an oil base; regular food coloring won't work.

Your butter will be much fresher and more nutritious than any you've ever purchased.

Experiment with both fresh cream and slightly soured cream in buttermaking. Both give a different taste. Commercial butter is generally made from cream which has been soured with a culture.

Storing butter for lengths of time
When you have plenty of cream, make extra butter to carry over while your animals are dry during the winter. There are two ways:
Freezing: Put fresh butter in a freezer container with a tight lid. Then wrap in moistureproof freezer wrap and store in your freezer. If done properly, the butter will keep for six months or more at 0°F. This butter must be made from pasteurized cream, or it may become rancid during the storage period.
Brining: Wrap each cube of butter in cloth and place in a scalded crock. Cover with brine consisting of a 10 percent salt solution, which will float a fresh egg. Weigh down the butter with a plate so that it's submerged in the brine. Butter stored in brine should keep all winter.

Cultured Dairy Foods

Foods made from cultures have existed for many centuries, often as staples of the diet. Some people, such as certain tribes in the Ural Mountains in western Asia, claim that cultured foods such as yogurt are the reason for their long lives. Of course, claims have linked longevity to innumerable factors. But it is true that culturing the milk makes it easy to digest because the resulting friendly bacteria and lactic acid are compatible with the digestive system. Many peoples around the world never use fresh milk—and in fact lose their ability to digest it—but do use cultured milk products.

Cultured foods contain specific living organisms which, used in a small quantity, will perpetuate the food almost indefinitely. In using a culture, it is necessary to remember to set aside a portion to use in starting the next batch.

Lactic acid, which helps keep the digestive system in good shape, results from the fermentation which occurs from culturing milk. For hundreds of years people throughout the world have supplied lactic acid to their diet through some form of cultured food, either in a food made with milk or some other way, such as with sauerkraut.

BUTTERMILK

Using the proper proportions of dry milk and water, mix **1 quart powdered skim milk**. Add **1 cup commercial buttermilk**. Let set overnight in a warm place. Next morning it will be ready. Just remember to save one cup for starting the next batch.

HOMEMADE SOUR CREAM

Mix: **1 pint heavy cream** and **2 tablespoons cultured buttermilk**. Let set at room temperature for 24 hours. Refrigerate 24 hours before use. It will keep a month.

COTTAGE CHEESE

Allow **skim milk** to set at about 70° for 24 hours. The curd should be firm enough to break cleanly when a finger inserted obliquely is pulled straight up. Cut the curd into small pieces as uniformly as possible.

Begin to heat in a double boiler, so that the temperature rises very slowly. When the curd pulls back from the container, begin stirring to prevent lumping.

Maintain the temperature at 105° until the curd is firm—from 15 to 30 minutes. A handful of curd washed in **cold water** should then have the desired appearance. The entire cooking time will be 1-1/2 to 2 hours.

Drain in a muslin bag above the sink, catching the whey to use as liquid in breadmaking. After draining, wash the cottage cheese three times in **cold water,** first at 70°, then at 55°, then in 40° **ice water.**

Salt if desired. Store in a cool place in a jar or crock. The cottage cheese will keep several days. The yield will be one-fifth to one-sixth the quantity of skim milk used.

CHEESE

When the animal is fresh, cheese is the traditional way to preserve the excess milk for the times when she is dry. The longer cheese sets, the better it gets.

Set **1 gallon of evening's milk** overnight in a cool place (about 50°). The next day, mix in **1 gallon of morning's milk.** Either goat's milk or cow's milk is fine, but the milk must not be sour.

Warm the milk in a stainless steel or enamel pan to 86°. Add **cheese coloring** if desired, obtained from a dairy supply house. Set the kettle in **a pail of warm water** (about 90°) and place in a draft-free warm place. Add **1/4 Hansen's rennet tablet** dissolved in **a glass of cold water.** Stir the milk thoroughly for 1 minute after the rennet is added.

Set undisturbed for 30 to 45 minutes until a firm curd forms. When the curd breaks clean, it is ready. Cut the curd, using a long knife which reaches the bottom of the pan. Make cuts vertically and cuts at an angle so that all the curd is cut into pieces 1 inch or less thick. (see illustration on page 54).

Stir the curd by hand for 15 minutes, stirring from the bottom up. Cut any larger pieces to conform to the 1-inch size.

Heat slowly for about an hour until the temperature reaches 102°. The heat should be applied to the outer bucket. Stir often with a wooden spoon to keep the curd from sticking together.

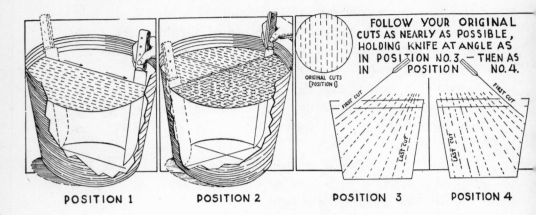

Cutting the curd.

At the end of the hour, the curd should hold its shape and fall apart when held in your hand.

Remove from the stove, but stir every few minutes to keep the curd from sticking together. Leave the curd in the whey until firm so the curd shakes apart when pressed in your hand. This step takes approximately 1 hour.

Pour into a 1-yard square of cheesecloth. Holding two corners of the cloth in each hand, roll the curd back and forth for 3 minutes until the whey has drained. Save the whey to use as liquid in making bread.

Put the cloth containing the curd into an empty kettle. Sprinkle in **2 tablespoons salt,** one at a time, mixing well without squeezing. Tie the four corners of the cloth together and hang above the sink to drip for 45 minutes.

Form the cheese into a round shape and encircle it with a cloth thickly folded into a 3-inch strip and pinned tightly around the cheese. The diameter of the cheese should be 6 inches or less.

Put several layers of cheesecloth above and below the cheese and cover the cheese with a board and a weight. That night, turn the cheese over and put on a heavier weight.

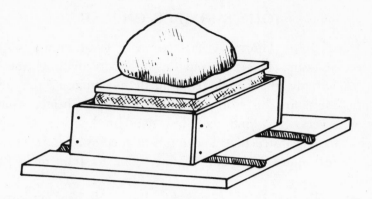

Next morning take the cloth from the cheese and let the cheese dry, turning occasionally, until a dry rind forms. Then dip in paraffin heated to 210°. Store in a clean, cool place, turning it daily for a few days, then several times a week.

Eat after a month if you wish, but the cheese will taste better as it ages longer.

A simple cheese press

Use a 2-pound coffee can, remove both ends from the can, and save them. Set one end in the bottom of the can. Mold the cheese to fit in the can, wrap it in cheese cloth, and place it in the can. Then place the other end of the can on top of the cheese. Place two bricks on top for weight.

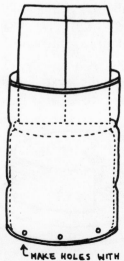

↖ MAKE HOLES WITH A NAIL FOR DRAINAGE

JOHN'S SIMPLE CHEESE

My friend John Thorndike farmed in a rural region of Chile for several years. There he and his neighbors made cheese every day, using only the simple equipment available in the peasant culture. Here are his instructions for a simple cheese, which he says was very good and took less than an hour to make. The cheese handling instructions above can be used as a guide. However, *this* cheese requires only one heating, done by John on a Primus stove.

Heat **milk** to 37° C. (78.5° F.). Turn off heat and sprinkle in **rennet,** using proportions in preceding recipe. The right amount of rennet will cause the curd to harden in 40 minutes. Cut the curd diagonally into 1-inch pieces as instructed above.

Then very gently break the curd apart with your hands. Gently dip out the whey. John says the local farmer who taught him always emphasized gentleness in handling the cheese.

Add **salt** (still using proportions of previous recipe) mixed in **a little hot water** and work in gently. Put the curd into a cheesecloth, working it into shape. Put the band of cheesecloth around the cheese and place in cheese press.

John's cheese press consisted of a bottom board, with grooves allowing the whey to drain; then the cheese form, made of 1- x 3-inch boards screwed together to form a square. In the sides were holes drilled to allow the whey to drain. The cheese in the cheesecloth was placed in the square open-ended box. Over the cheese was placed a square of wood slightly smaller than the inside dimensions of the box. This was weighted down with a rock. John feels the wooden press contributed to the flavor of the cheese and was also more aesthetic than a metal press.

Remove cheese from press the next day and dip in **paraffin.** This cheese is good after three weeks; it is hard in three months.

RENNET

Rennet is commonly made from the mucuous membrane of the last or "true" stomach (abomasum) of a calf. During butchering in former times this stomach was saved specifically for cheesemaking. This stomach is also called the rennet for the active ingredient, rennin, which it contains. The rennet was either used fresh or was salted and dried for later use. Rennet or rennet liquor was added to the milk in cheesemaking. Rennet liquor was made by leaving a small quantity of the calf stomach in a small amount of water overnight.

Sometimes in remote or poor areas where rennet wasn't available, old cheese was mixed into a paste with bread and water. The mixture was put into a cheesecloth and hung until dry. Then a small bit of the dried mixture was dissolved in water and added to the milk in place of rennet.

It has been suggested that the cooking liquor of stinging nettle or sundew (*Drosera*) works as a vegetable rennet for milk. However, to my knowledge its value in cheesemaking is not confirmed.

Several types of commercial rennet are available today.

YOGURT

All yogurt begins with yogurt or yogurt starter. The yogurt is obtained from a yogurt-making friend or purchased as a commercial yogurt starter. Sometimes plain commercial yogurt will work as a starter, sometimes not, depending on its quality.

Yogurt is a pleasing and economical way to obtain B vitamins. Also, the bacteria present in yogurt are beneficial to digestion. These bacteria are of the type normally found in the intestinal tract that aid digestion and help prevent the putrefaction of food. The beneficial bacteria found in the intestinal tract can be destroyed by the use of some antibiotics, and at such a time the proper bacterial balance can be restored by yogurt.

The two most common types of yogurt are *bulgaricus* and

acidophilus, the names of the culturing organisms. The most easily obtainable yogurt and yogurt starter is the *bulgaricus* type.

Acidophilus is closer to the type of organism found naturally in the human body's digestive system, but it is more difficult to obtain. *L. acidophilus* culture produces conditions unfavorable to harmful bacteria and assists in the synthesis of folic acid and vitamin K. It aids digestion and destroys waste toxins.

Serve yogurt cold and plain, or topped with fruit and/or honey. The fruit or honey may be mixed into the yogurt after setting, but I have not found success in mixing in anything extra before the yogurt sets.

Below are methods for making yogurt from both dry powdered milk and fresh milk. I prefer to make yogurt from dry powdered milk, as it is simpler and not as temperamental, but either way will work well. It just depends on your preference and the raw materials available.

YOGURT MADE WITH DRY POWDERED MILK

This makes about 1 quart of finished yogurt and costs very little. It's low in calories. Use as little as **1/2 cup dry skim milk,** or as much as **2-2/3 cups dry skim milk.** Use the lesser amount if you want a liquid yogurt, the greater amount for a custardy yogurt. Add **3-3/4 cups water** at room temperature. Beat. Then stir in thoroughly or blend **3 generous tablespoons yogurt.** Pour into glass casseroles or jars. Cover. The yogurt must not touch metal. Keep at a temperature of 100° to 105°. A constant temperature is very important. The yogurt will be firm in 8 to 12 hours and will get firmer the longer it sets. After you've used your starter a while, the time required to firm will become less.

Before refrigerating be sure to set aside 3 tablespoons of yogurt in a little jar as a starter for the next batch. Do this before you refrigerate so it won't accidently be eaten.

BILL'S YOGURT MADE WITH WHOLE MILK

Scald **1 quart milk,** being careful not to boil it. Add **1/2 cup dry powdered milk.** Cool rapidly to 105°. Add **3 tablespoons**

starter. Set at 105° to 110°. The first batch will take about 8 hours; eventually the yogurt will set in 3 to 4 hours. Remember to set aside 3 tablespoons for next time before eating.

YOGURT DRINK

Shake together **2 cups thick yogurt** and **1 cup pure cherry juice** (or other juice). A delicious, healthful drink!

CREAM CHEESE

In a cheesecloth above the kitchen sink, hang **1 cup homemade yogurt** with a bowl underneath to catch the dripping whey for breadmaking. Let drip overnight. Next morning—presto! cream cheese.

TOPPING OR DIP

Yogurt can be used as a topping for baked potatoes in place of sour cream. Use plain, or add **chopped chives.**

Use as a dip by adding **chopped onions, garlic powder,** and/or **chili powder** to taste. Experiment with different seasonings.

A yogurt maker to provide constant heat
The more consistent your heat source, the more successful you will become at yogurtmaking. Here are some suggestions:

1. The simplest and most expensive heat source is a purchased yogurt maker. This consists of a thermostatically controlled plastic plate on which you set the glass dishes that come with the yogurt maker. The cost is $10 to $15. Generally obtainable at health-food stores.
2. For myself, I've devised a simple and easily obtainable yogurt maker, free or at small cost. It has served me well. Obtain an old electric frying pan or deep-fat fryer, if you don't already have one. Visit rummage sales and Goodwill to find one. It can be ugly and pitted as long as the thermostat works; your yogurt will never touch its surface.

Put a quart of water in the appliance and plug it in. Turn the temperature setting slightly above "on." Let an aquarium thermometer float on the water. Adjust the control until the water temperature holds between 100° and 105°. Make a mark on the control at that point with fingernail polish or paint. You now have a thermostatically controlled yogurt maker.

Use by setting low casserole dishes in shallow water in the frying pan, or by setting jars in shallow water in the deep-fat fryer. The water will help distribute the heat evenly.

3. Buy a small aquarium heater (cost about $4) and set it in a pan of water to give a constant temperature. Place jars of yogurt in the resulting warm water after you have followed the procedure in the above paragraph to find and mark the correct temperature setting.

4. You can use your oven to give consistent heat. Preheat the oven to 105°, using a thermometer to check the temperature. Maintain heat at 105°. (Some gas ovens are kept at that temperature by their pilot lights.) Your oven may hold at the proper temperature for the time it takes the yogurt to set, or you may have to turn it on briefly once in a while.

5. Wrap the jars in an electric heating pad checked and set for the proper temperature.

6. A more difficult method is to heat a deep pan of water to 110° on top of the kitchen range. Maintain heat at 105°. Insert the jars of yogurt and cover the pan. This method will require keeping a frequent watch on the temperature and turning on the heat from time to time. Improvements on this method are to put the heated pan of water containing the jars of yogurt into a styrofoam cooler with a tight lid; or to wrap the heated pan containing the yogurt in a blanket.

7. Rig a device using a styrofoam cooler and a small light bulb on an extension cord. Just be sure the bulb is moored tightly to prevent fire hazard.

8. Put yogurt mix at proper temperature into a thermos bottle.

9. Use an electric hot tray. Test temperature according to procedure given above. If temperature is too high, add a folded towel between tray and yogurt to decrease temperature.

Eggs

Organic eggs are a fine food; eggs from large egg farms are not so good. There the chickens never leave their little cages, see sunlight, or touch the ground. Often hens raised under such conditions are urged to lay larger quantities by being fed amphetamines and hormones with their chemicalized rations. They certainly wouldn't lay well out of happiness!

If you've never had one, a Real Egg is a treat. It's best to get eggs from your own chickens who scratch in the dirt and eat organic rations and insects from the yard. Real Eggs vary in flavor according to what forage is available. Yolks of spring eggs are usually orange. In some places marigold petals have been mixed with the chicken feed to brighten the yolks. Nutritionally, fertile eggs may be superior, so you'll want to keep a good rooster.

If you can't grow your own hens, find a farmer, health-food store, or co-op that does offer organic eggs.

If you've got hens, you'll find you will have many more eggs

in the spring than you do in the winter. So during the productive times, or when eggs are cheapest to purchase, store excess eggs for the lean times. Nonfertile eggs store best.

FREEZING EGGS

Wash eggs in cool water. Break each egg separately and examine it to be sure it's fresh. Package the eggs (without shells) according to your need; i.e., six eggs per package or whatever you're most likely to use. Leave a little space in the moistureproof container for expansion from freezing. Label each package with the date and quantity of eggs. Freeze. They'll keep six to eight months at 0°.

Never wash eggs when storing in the shell. They come direct from the hen with a protective coating which seals in the freshness. It is enough to wipe them with a dry cloth.

CROCKED DRY STORAGE

My great-grandmother used this method. The first step is optional.

Dip eggs in warm mineral oil and let dry. This seals shells, but Grandma skipped it. She began with the next step.

Into a crock, place a layer of wheat or other small grain. Then place a layer of eggs on top of the grain. Pour grain over and around the layer of eggs, covering well. Alternate layers of eggs and grain. Cover to keep out rodents. Place the crock in a cool, dry cellar, and the eggs will keep all winter. The grain acts as insulation and helps maintain proper humidity and cushioning for the eggs.

EGG PASTA AS STORAGE

A sensible and convenient method to keep eggs for later use is to make pasta from the eggs as they accumulate. The dry pasta will keep a long time in tight jars in a cool place. See recipes given in the section on *Pasta*.

PICKLED EGGS

Carefully shell **15 to 18 hard-boiled eggs.** Place them in hot, sterilized jars and cover with the following boiling solution:

3 cups vinegar
1 cup water
1 teaspoon salt
pickling spices (if desired)

Seal immediately with hot, sterilized lids. The eggs will keep indefinitely.

BRINING EGGS

This old method will reputedly keep eggs two years or more! It was often used by general stores and on board ships.

Gently place washed eggs in a crock. Cover with a well-mixed solution of **3 gallons water, 1 pint slacked lime** (quicklime, from lumber yards), and **1 cup salt.** Cover with a board or plate topped by a rock to hold eggs under the brine. Place a little lime and salt on the board to maintain a consistent solution throughout the crock. When adding eggs, lower them in a dish until the dish fills with brine, then gently roll the eggs out so they won't crack.

And how to use those dozens of fresh eggs when the hens are so prolific in the spring? Add eggs to many things to improve flavor and protein content. Stir in an egg with sautéed vegetables. Instead of regular fruit pies, make fruit custard pies. (See *Desserts.*) Whip up an eggnog after work or after school. Make your own mayonnaise. (See *Salads.*) Add an extra egg or two in custards and cakes and bread.

EGG CUSTARD

This custard recipe can be made to accommodate the number of eggs you have available by varying the proportions from 1 egg per each cup of milk to 2 eggs per each cup of milk.

Mix the following:

2 cups milk	1/3 cup brown sugar
3 eggs	1/8 teaspoon nutmeg
1 teaspoon vanilla	1/8 teaspoon cinnamon
1/8 teaspoon salt	

Pour into either 4 custard cups or a one-quart casserole. Set in a pan of water. Bake in 350⁰ oven until golden and firm, about 40 minutes for small custard cups; about 70 minutes for casserole dish. When done, a silver knife inserted comes away clean. The more eggs used, the higher the custard will rise. Serves 4.

Variation

For *rice* or *noodle pudding,* add **up to 2 cups leftover rice or noodles.** Add **1/2 cup raisins,** if desired.

OMELETTE

Beat lightly **6 eggs.** Mix in:

1 cup milk	1 teaspoon rosemary
2 tablespoons flour	1 clove garlic, crushed
1 cup chopped, mixed vegetables (onions, green peppers, celery, olives, mushrooms, whatever you have)	1/2 cup ham or crisp bacon bits
	2/3 cup Cheddar or longhorn cheese, chunks or grated
1 tablespoon oregano	salt and pepper to taste

Preheat cast-iron skillet at medium heat with suffcent cooking oil to cover pan's bottom. Pour in mixture and cover with lid. Turn heat to low. Check omelette in about 20 minutes; it is ready when golden on bottom and firm on top. Serve as is, or slide out of pan and fold over. Just remember, if you keep removing the lid to peek, the omelette will loose its puffiness. Serves 4.

MATZO BREI

Beat together (per person to be served):

1 egg

1 crushed garlic or onion matzo, or regular soda cracker (4 squares)

Salt and pepper to taste

Let mixture soak together for 1/2 hour. Then fry in preheated cast-iron skillet. For variation, before frying add **1 tablespoon chopped onion** and **1 tablespoon chopped mushrooms.**

EASTER EGGS

When I was growing up, my grandmother made organic Easter eggs. They were all one color, but they were beautiful. In an enamel or stainless steel pan (no aluminum if you use vinegar), boil **eggs** in water to which **1 tablespoon vinegar** and **dried peels from red onions** are added. These are a beautiful burgundy to deep red in color. Try yellow onion peels for a pale gold.

Seed Sprouting

If you dwell in the tiniest of apartments on the twenty-fifth floor of a metropolitan building, you can still grow some of your own vegetables winter and summer. Yes, anyone can grow one of the most nutritious vegetables available anywhere in any quantity they desire. The cost? A couple of cents a pound at most.

The particular vegetable I have in mind is sprouted seeds—mung bean, alfalfa, wheat, soybean, lentil—whatever you choose. Almost any seeds can be sprouted for food.

The advantages of seed sprouting include:

• *Great nutritional value.* Sprouted seeds are tremendously richer in vitamins, minerals, enzymes, and protein than unsprouted seeds or ordinary vegetables. Vitamins A and C particularly are produced in great quantities. Sprouted legumes and grains provide enough first-class proteins to be considered complete.

• *Space saving.* Enough seeds for sprouting for the entire year can be stored in a very small space. Only 3 tablespoons of mung bean seeds will make 1 quart of fresh bean sprouts, and seeds take up very little room while sprouting.

● *Economy.* Most seeds used in sprouting are relatively inexpensive, a pound of home-grown fresh sprouts costs much less than a pound of purchased vegetables.

● *Diet variety.* Sprouts can be used in a variety of ways; for example, raw in salads or cooked in soups. Mung bean sprouts are especially good stirred into scrambled eggs or omelettes. They can be mixed with sandwich spread. They can be sautéed as a green vegetable.

● *Simplicity.* You probably have the equipment now to be able to sprout seeds at home.

● *Convenience.* Seeds can be sprouted in any home. Assure yourself of fresh vegetables on that camping trip by taking along some seeds for sprouting. Do the initial overnight soaking while at your campsite. They'll grow fine in the back cupboard in the van or in the side pocket of your pack.

Begin with an ordinary canning or mayonnaise jar, a 4-inch square of nylon net, a screw ring that fits the jar, and a lid.

Put 3 tablespoons of seeds or beans into the jar and fill halfway with water. Cover with the regular tight lid. Let set overnight. Next morning remove lid; replace with netting and screw ring. Pour the water out through the netting. Put fresh water over the seeds, swirl, and pour off the water completely. Set the container in a dark place. Each morning rinse the seeds with fresh water in the same manner. After three or four days, when the little sprouts are an inch long, place the container in the sun. Continue to rinse daily with cold water.

Tiny leaves will form, and the sprouts will turn green. The sprouts are then ready to eat or to store in the refrigerator or freezer. Eat the refrigerated sprouts as quickly as possible for the best nutritional value. The exception to this rule is soybean sprouts. They reach their full nutritional potential after almost a week of refrigeration.

Sprouts are good raw. They are sweeter if sautéed in a little oil. Fortify vegetable soup by adding 1 to 2 cups of sprouts during the last 5 minutes of simmering.

The following recipes are extremely inexpensive and serve five people or more generously.

EGG FOO YONG

Heat a little **oil** in a cast-iron pan. Beat **6 eggs**. Stir in **1 cup sprouts**. Pour into pan to make 4-inch cakes and cook on both sides until brown. Or pour into pan and stir to scramble. Serve topped with **soy sauce or tamari**.

SPROUT SALAD

Chop:

1 avocado	1/2 onion
1 green pepper	1 cup fresh mushrooms
2 tomatoes	

Add **2 cups fresh sprouts**. Toss together and add **mayonnaise** or your favorite mild salad dressing.

SPROUT SANDWICH SPREAD

Chop:

6 boiled eggs	1/2 cup fresh mushrooms
1/2 onion	1 15-ounce can mackerel
1 pickle	

Add **2 cups sprouts**. Stir together. Add **mayonnaise** to proper spreading consistency. Serve on good **whole-grain bread**.

Growing Mushrooms

If you enjoy fresh mushrooms, but find the price out of sight, consider growing them at home. I have grown mushrooms under my kitchen sink. A basement, cave, garage, or barn will work also. Mushrooms can be grown at a range of temperatures, as long as extreme heat or freezing are avoided. Temperatures of 70° to 80° work best. A high humidity can be maintained by using polyethylene tents to cover your growing boxes.

First, you must compost the growing medium. One suggested mixture consists of: **40% hay or straw, 40% sawdust,** and **20% animal manure.** The animal manure is essential, preferably from horses or chickens.

The next step, which is optional, is to bake the growing medium in your oven at 200° for 1 hour. This should kill any stray life in the compost, such as other mushroom spawn or seeds. However, if the composting mixture has heated up well, this won't be necessary.

Next, find a heavy, waxed cardboard box of the appropriate size, or build a wooden box. The box should be 5 or 6 inches deep.

If you wish to grow large quantities, shelves or racks may be built to hold the growing boxes. A rack may be constructed like this, with growing boxes that slide in and out. Encase the entire rack in a polyethylene tent (see illustration on page 69).

Obtain edible mushroom spawn from a seed company, such as Gurney's Seeds of Yankton, South Dakota. You can purchase enough spawn for 12 square feet for about a dollar. Seed companies also sell mushroom-growing kits, an interesting experiment for beginners.

It is necessary to purchase spawn. Even if you know wild mushrooms well, you will not be able to duplicate the sensitive growing conditions they require.

Fill the growing box with the composted medium. Sprinkle in some spawn. Cover thinly with compost. Sprinkle gently with warm water, about a half cup per square foot. Place a plastic sheet over the box like a tent, allowing a little ventilation.

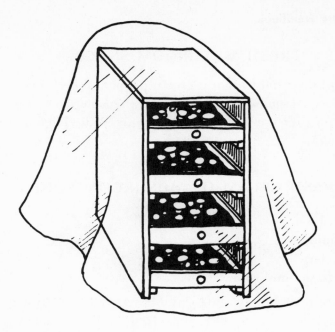

Water two or three times weekly; make certain the soil doesn't dry out and isn't spongy wet. After three weeks, or after the first sign of life, add a half inch of loose compost. In four to six weeks, you'll have your first crop.

Harvest. Then sprinkle on an additional inch of composted mixture and repeat the process. After three or four crops you will have to fix an entirely new boxful of potting compost, as the nutrients in the soil will be depleted. The old mixture will be good humus; spread it on your garden or potted plants.

Mushrooms are so much better fresh, and they're right there when you need them if you grow your own. Nutritionally, they contain some vitamin D and several of the B vitamins, plus hard-to-obtain folic acid and several minerals, especially iron and copper.

Growing mushrooms at home can also provide a good income. Arrangements can be made for local sale of fresh mushrooms or mail-order sales of dried mushrooms.

Mushrooms can be kept by drying, freezing, or canning (pressure canner method). Drying is by far the easiest and most convenient. Just slice the mushrooms thin and dry them on racks in your oven at 170° until brittle. One pound of dry mushrooms is equivalent to five to seven pounds of fresh mushrooms. Reconstitute by soaking in water, or add dry mushrooms directly to soup.

FRESH MUSHROOM SNACK

Mix **fresh, raw mushrooms, green pepper slices,** and **cheese chunks** in equal portions. A great midafternoon snack. Or serve it as an appetizer, or add as a garnish to salads. High nutrition and low calorie.

FRESH CREAM OF MUSHROOM SOUP

Finely chop:

1 cup onion
1 cup celery
4 cups fresh mushrooms

Sauté mixture **in butter.** Add **2 tablespoons flour.** Brown and stir until golden. Add **6 to 8 cups fresh milk.** Season to taste.

Simmer gently on low heat for 1/2 hour. Watch heat carefully so the milk doesn't scorch. Serve hot, with **Cheddar cheese** grated on top.

Mushrooms are also delicious in your favorite omelette—or sautéed with dinner vegetable.

IN THE
NITTY GRITTY KITCHEN

Breakfasts

Be good to yourself until 10 A.M. and the rest of the day will take care of itself.

Begin your day with a good, nourishing breakfast you've made. These breakfasts can all be prepared in advance, so there need be no last-minute rush. They are easy to fix and as quick as packaged cereal, yet the cost is but a fraction of purchased breakfasts and the nutritional value much greater. They all use versatile ingredients that you're likely to have on hand for other things.

HOT CRACKED GRAIN

The most basic cereal and the cheapest is a cooked grain cereal. The cost is under one cent per serving.

Grind your grain, wheat for example, at a coarse setting, so the result is cracked wheat rather than flour.

Cook **1/2 cup cracked grain** per person in **boiling water** (to which **a dash of salt** has been added) until soft, 20 minutes to 1/2 hour, simmering and stirring as it begins to thicken. Add **dried fruit or raisins** if desired. Serve with **milk and honey**.

SUSAN'S PANCAKES

I first sampled these pancakes on a camping trip, and they took my breath away on that chilly morning in those beautiful woods. The dry ingredients had been mixed together in advance, and the batter was whipped up by the first people who struggled out of their tent.

Mix together well:

1 cup rye flour	2 eggs
2 cups whole-wheat flour	1-1/2 cups milk (more if
1 teaspoon baking powder	thinner pancakes are
1 teaspoon salt	desired, less for thicker
1/4 cup raw sesame seeds	ones)

Ladle a half cup at a time onto a hot, greased griddle. Serves 4 or 5.

FAMILIA

Familia is the real all-purpose convenience food. No mix whipped together by the food hucksters is as nourishing or versatile. Because of the nuts and dry fruits the total cost of mixing up a batch may seem high, but if you figure the cost per pound and then compare the pound cost of packaged puffaway cereals, you'll find the cost of Familia the same or less.

Familia can be as simple or as elaborate as you wish. It can be eaten dry, making it an ideal food to take along on a hike. Or it can be served with milk or water as a hot or cold cereal. The same mix is also the basic ingredient for cookies and hot cakes. Familia can also be stored in a moistureproof container for quite a length of time.

Familia is usually made with half cereal, half fruit and nuts. This recipe is one of those allowing you a free artistic hand, so do what you will with it according to your desire and what you have on hand. As a simple rule of thumb, simply use **one-half cereal, one-fourth fruit,** and **one-fourth nuts,** plus **dry powdered milk, sugar,** and **wheat germ** if desired. Just remember, too much wheat germ or raw sunflower seeds will make the cereal bitter.

FAMILIA

Large batch (about 17 pounds)/smaller batch (5 quarts):

8 pounds / 8 cups rolled oats
1 pound / 1 cup raisins
1 pound / 1 cup currants
1 pound / 1 cup roasted peanuts
1 pound / 1 cup raw cashews
1 pound / 1 cup raw almonds
1 pound / 1 cup roasted sunflower seeds
1/2 pound / 1/2 cup sesame seeds
1 pound / 1 cup dry apricots
1 pound / 1 cup dry apples
1 cup / 1/4 cup wheat germ
5 cups / 2 cups dry powdered milk
2 cups / 1 cup brown sugar

Mix ingredients by shaking in a large, double grocery bag. Store in a large, tight container or several smaller ones.

Serve hot by simmering required amount in a little water. Or for instant hot cereal, pour a little boiling water over Familia in a bowl. For cold cereal, add a little cold milk or cold water and fresh fruit if desired.

TIM'S FAMILIA HOTCAKES

One day, feeling creative and hungry, my son Tim created these easy, scrumptious hotcakes, and quick enough to catch the school bus.

Beat (per person to be served) **1 egg** with **2 tablespoons milk.** Add **Familia** until mixture is stiff. Beat together well. Spoon onto hot, oiled, heavy griddle and cook until golden on both sides. Good served with **maple syrup, honey, or homemade fruit syrup.**

TIM'S DELUXE FAMILIA HOTCAKES

Make Familia hotcakes as above. Top with **yogurt** and **fresh strawberries,** or **blueberries.** Good for breakfast or dessert.

FAMILIA COOKIES

To about **8 cups Familia mix** add **1 egg** and **1/2 cup oil**. Mix well. If dough is too stiff, add water to make the desired consistency. Drop small balls of the mixture on a greased cookie sheet. Bake at 350° for about 12 minutes, or until golden brown.

FAMILIA BREAD

Vary **Nitty Gritty Bread** (see page 79) by omitting 1 cup flour and adding **1 cup Familia mix** to the batch. Continue as usual. This is good toasted.

FAMILIA SNACK

Keep dry Familia mix on hand for camping trips and for after work and school snacks. Send the kiddies out to play with Baggies of Familia mix clenched in their little fists.

Your family will not tire of Familia if you vary the ingredients. I do this by adding ingredients as the container begins to empty, mixing and keeping the same approximate proportions. Use fruits and nuts different from the preceeding batch. The dry fruits used should preferably be organic and preserved without sulphur. Your favorite Familia will gradually evolve.

CRUNCHY GRANOLA

Granola, like Familia, varies considerably from household to household. Here is a basic recipe which you'll probably alter to suit your taste. Granola differs from Familia in that its original mix is toasted. Yields about 12 cups.

6 cups rolled oats	**1 cup slivered almonds**
1 cup wheat germ	**1 cup sunflower seeds**
1 cup sesame seeds	**1/2 cup oil**
1-1/2 cups coconut	

Heat the oil in a heavy pan. Mix ingredients together, then dump in pan. Add **1/2 cup honey** and **1 teaspoon vanilla.** Stir and heat until browned and slightly clumped together. Or pour into a pan and bake for 20 minutes at 350⁰, stirring frequently.

Cool, break into spoon-size pieces, and store. Serve with milk.

HOMEMADE GRAPENUT-LIKE CEREAL

Sift together **3-1/2 cups graham flour** and **1 cup brown sugar.** Add and mix together thoroughly **1 teaspoon soda** and **1 teaspoon salt.** Add **2 cups buttermilk** or **sour milk.** Beat until smooth.

Spread dough 1/4 inch thick on greased cookie sheets. Bake at 375⁰ for about 15 minutes or until crisp and golden brown. Let cool thoroughly. Grind in a food chopper or through a flour mill at coarse setting. Or roll the pieces with a rolling pin until crumbled. Crisp in oven before serving, if desired. Serve with milk. Yields about 4-1/2 cups.

Other Nitty Gritty breakfasts I suggest include Sourdough Pancakes (see page 91), fresh yogurt with fruit (see page 58), and Sourdough Brunch (see page 113). I myself usually have a high protein breakfast of real eggs, a slice of Nitty Gritty Bread, and fresh fruit and milk. Or sometimes fresh egg custard, fruit, and good cocoa or herb tea.

Breads

During much of man's history, bread was the food which sustained him. Since the advent of overcommercialized packaged flours and then loaves of packaged bread during the last century, breads have gradually ceased to be the healthful life-sustainers they should be. As industrial milling of grains advanced, flours became less nutritious, until now most flours are but ghosts of their former selves. With the intense milling, bleaching, and preserving processes, most of the B vitamins and vitamin E are destroyed. The chemicals

are added to return some of what was removed and destroyed, and the flour or bread comes to you in a package marked "enriched."

The way out?

It's fairly simple to assure yourself and your family of good bread—by baking it yourself.

Whole-grain flours are generally available in health-food stores, and sometimes at your grocery if you look carefully and pay more.

Or, if you have the time and desire, it's simple and extremely economical to grind your own. Hand-operated mills are available for about $15. The two I would suggest are Quaker and Corona. The Corona seems to be sturdier, but the Quaker gives finer flour in one milling. I usually put the grain through my Corona twice to get fine flour.

If you purchase a grinder, you will need a strong, stable surface to which to attach it, preferably a permanent place. Grinding the grain for a batch of bread doesn't take much time, but it does take some energy, especially if you are accustomed to an all-electric kitchen. But it's a meaningful form of exercise—great for flabby arms, sagging chest, and weak stomach muscles! You can buy an electric mill, but it will cost over $100.

Where do you get the whole grain?

The first choice is to grow it yourself, if you have the time and land available.

If you have access to farmers, they would be the second choice. But ask the farmer how he grew the grain. Did he use chemical fertilizers or pesticides? Generally, in more depressed farming areas, he will not. Maybe he doesn't do organic farming, but economically he simply can't afford all those chemicals. Gladly pay his price for his good food and effort—he's earned it. The farmer will sell by the bushel, and a bushel of wheat weighs approximately 60 pounds.

The third choice for whole grains would be a health-food store. It will assure you that the grain was organically grown, but the price will be much higher—probably three to five times the cost of the whole grain purchased directly from the farmer.

Fourth choice would be a feed store, where you go to buy animal feeds. Here you have no assurance of how the grain was grown. However, any residues from sprays are likely to be in powder form, which can mostly be removed by washing. Use a sieve; do not soak in water. Spread to dry. Be sure all grains are totally dry before storing, to prevent spoilage, and before running through your mill, to prevent a gummy mess. But absolutely *do not buy seed grains for food,* as they are heavily treated with chemicals. Buy grains that would ordinarily be mixed for animal feed, rather than seed. At a feed store your hundredweight should cost about one and a half to twice the farmer's price.

If none of these possibilities for buying grain is available to you, you might mail order. (See *Directory of Sources.*)

What are the advantages of grinding the grain yourself?

1. The savings are immense.
2. Each grain is a nutritionally sealed unit before grinding. When you grind, you get the fresh nutritional value intact—the vitamins are there, the wheat germ is there, and the natural oil is still fresh and hasn't been treated with preservatives to keep it from becoming rancid.
3. You can custom-blend your flour. For example, you can mix several cups of wheat, rye, and rice; add some nuts or sunflower seeds; and perhaps even add clean egg shells from your own organic chickens for extra calcium.

Many health-food stores grind their own grains, so their flour should be quite fresh. Packaged whole-grain flours found on the shelf in the health-food store or grocery store will be considerably older, but are still an incredible improvement over white, bleached, enriched plastic flour.

Whole-grain breads do tend to be coarser than white-flour breads.

I have found that my family prefers unbleached flour to comprise one-third to one-half the quantity of flour used in baking simply because it improves the texture and appearance. Unbleached flour has neither been bleached nor enriched; because it is not enriched, it should not be used as the only flour. It can be obtained from some health-food stores or by the hundredweight from some bakeries. It is available from some groceries, also.

In place of unbleached flour, you can use whole-wheat pastry flour, which has a fine texture.

Home-ground flours tend to be coarser than whole-grain flours that you buy. Of course, your mill is adjustable. But the finer the grind, the harder the grinding.

When baking with whole-grain flours, you must knead the dough a little longer to work the gluten free—that's what holds the bread together and gives it texture.

To know the bread you must first know its parts, so here are some hints about ingredients:

Yeast. One cake, packet, or tablespoon raises 3 to 8 cups of flour, depending on how heavy the dough is, how fresh the yeast is, the altitude, and the weather. The heavier the flour, the more yeast required. The higher the altitude, the less yeast required. Yeast is a living organism and so is very sensitive to conditions, particularly heat and cold. Treat it with care.

Liquid. Use water, milk, potato water, mu or spice tea—1 cup liquid to 3 or 4 cups flour.

Honey or sugar. Activates the yeast, browns the crust, and adds flavor.

Ginger. Helps the yeast action and adds mild flavor.

Salt. For flavor, stabilization of fermentation, and preservation, use 1 teaspoon to 2 cups flour.

Shortening. Can be lard, margarine, or butter; if you use oil, use about half the amount. (The recipe below gives the proper quantity of oil.)

Following are some healthful substitutes:

Substitute honey for white sugar as a first choice; brown sugar for white sugar as a second choice. Substitute an equal amount of brown sugar; the quantity of honey substituted should be from half to an amount equal to the white sugar.

Substitute cold-pressed vegetable oils for lard or shortening. Half the quantity is usually used. Cold-pressed oils are best as they have retained more of their natural nutrients because they have not been refined with heat. In pastry, like pie crust, lard creates a better texture than oil.

Substitute carob for cocoa in an equal amount. Carob powder is rich in B vitamins and not harmful like chocolate. The result will taste slightly different than chocolate, but delicious. If you are "hooked" on chocolate, try using half chocolate, half carob.

Substitute sea salt for regular table salt. The sea salt should be without magnesium carbonate, which is often added to commercial salt. Magnesium carbonate is added to keep the salt from lumping due to moisture, but really doesn't do your body any good. Sea salt contains helpful trace minerals. Perhaps it might be said that sea salt is nearer the makeup of the human body, which is 98 percent water.

Substitute sunflower seeds for nuts. If your recipe calls for nuts but your budget doesn't, substitute an equal amount of roasted or raw sunflower seeds, an excellent source of vitamin E. Raw nuts are more healthful than roasted nuts. Raw peanuts (a legume, not a nut) and sunflower seeds are slightly bitter; roasted may taste better to you.

Decide for yourself how much you are willing to change your diet to eat more nutritiously.

Here's how to make 3 or 4 loaves of:

NITTY GRITTY BREAD

Into a very large bowl, pour **4-1/2 cups warm water**, a little cooler than your wrist—about 80° to 85°. Add: **4 tablespoons dry powdered yeast** (or 4 packets, or 4 cakes), **1/3 cup honey, or 1/2 cup brown sugar, 1 tablespoon ginger**. Stir until the yeast is well-dissolved. Then add **4 cups unbleached flour**. Mix well, then ignore for half an hour while you grind your whole-grain flour or do something else. During this time the yeast will begin to work, getting a head start toward expanding all that heavy whole-grain flour you're going to add soon.

Next add:

2 eggs
2 tablespoons salt
1/2 cup oil
1 cup dry milk powder

(If you wish to add whole milk, it must be scalded, and you decrease the liquid by the amount of whole milk added.)

Mix well. Add:

5 cups whole-wheat flour	or	4 cups whole wheat flour
5 cups rye flour		4 cups rye flour
		2 cups soy flour

or any other flour mixture you choose, to bring the total to approximately 14 cups. Mix the flour and knead in until the dough feels similar to the consistency of your earlobe. If you add too much flour, the bread will be coarse and dry. It should be sticky enough to pick up the flour from the bowl, but not sticky enough to be hard to handle with your oiled hands.

Now work the dough on a lightly floured board. Knead it by folding over toward you, then pressing away with the heels of your hands. Turn the dough around a little, then repeat the kneading. Repeat until the dough is not sticky, but is smooth and elastic. Place in a greased bowl for rising, turning the dough over once so the greased side is up to prevent a hard crust from forming.

Cover the dough and let it rise. The place you choose should

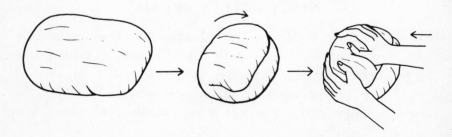

be 80° to 85° and without a draft. If you have a gas range, the pilot light in the oven will provide the right temperature. If your stove is electric, turn on the oven and let it warm slightly at the lowest temperature. Then turn off the oven and put in the dough to rise with the oven door slightly open. But watch the temperature carefully—if it's too cool, the yeast won't grow; if it's too warm, the heat will kill the yeast.

Let the dough rise until double in size, but no more. Otherwise it will fall and become coarse and dry when baked. The time needed for doubling the size will vary according to temperature, altitude, and consistency of the dough, but it will be about 45 minutes to 2 hours. Dough rises faster the higher the altitude. A finger pressed into the dough will leave an indentation when the dough has doubled.

Now punch down the dough: Push your fist into the dough, bring the edges into the center, and turn the dough over in the bowl. Let it rise again until almost double, about 15 to 45 minutes.

Now cut the dough with a knife into three or four pieces for molding into loaves. Let rise another 10 minutes. Set the oven to preheat at 350° (sea level) or 400° (above 4,000 feet) while you are preparing the loaves.

With closed fists work the air out of each portion with a rolling motion. Work and roll each portion into a loaf shape. Place the dough in your greased bread pan with the edge where the loaf comes together toward the bottom of the pan. The pan should be two-thirds full.

Cover the loaves with a cloth, and let them rise outside the oven until the dough reaches the tops of the pans and the middle of the loaf is rounded (about 30 to 60 minutes). A slight indentation will be left with the finger when the loaves are ready to bake.

Place the pans in the center of the hot oven, allowing space between them for the heat to circulate. Bake until brown (about 40 to 50 minutes). Tap the loaves out of the pans. If baked throughout, the loaves will sound hollow when you tap their bottoms. If not done, return loaves to the oven for a few minutes.

Take the bread from the pans and set it to cool sideways across the pans. Spread a thin coating of oil on the crusts with a pastry brush and then cover the loaves with a cloth or wax paper, if you desire a soft crust. Do not oil or cover if you want them crisp. Let cool thoroughly, then store the bread in a metal, ventilated breadbox. If you put the loaves in tight plastic bags while warm, they will mold if kept at room temperature. If the bread will be used slowly, keep it fresh in the refrigerator, placing it in plastic bags after cooling thoroughly. Store the bread you won't use within two or three days in the freezer. Reheat in a paper bag sprinkled with water in a 400⁰ oven for 10 minutes or until thawed.

You can also freeze the unbaked loaves of dough. Bake them later after allowing to thaw and rise. The quality will be better, however, if baked and then frozen.

Fresh bread is best cut with a serrated knife, using a sawing motion. In any case, make sure your knife is sharp, and saw—rather than pressing downward—with the knife.

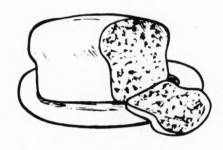

KAREN'S PARTY BREAD

A sweet dessert in itself.

Dissolve **1 tablespoon yeast** in **1/4 cup warm water** and set aside. Scald **1/2 cup milk** and pour into a large bowl. Add **2/3 cup sugar, 1/4 teaspoon salt,** and **1/4 cup butter.** Cool to luke-warm. Add **3 eggs,** one at a time. Beat until blended. Mix in yeast and **1 teaspoon grated lemon peel.** Gradually beat in **3 cups flour,** then add enough additional flour to make a soft dough.

Knead until smooth and springy, about 10 minutes. Let rise 2 hours, until double. Knead lightly again. Shape into an angel-food cake pan, about 9 inches in diameter and buttered. Let rise again until double. Brush top with **1 egg white.** Sprinkle with **3 tablespoons sugar.** Bake at 350⁰ for 45 minutes. Cool and serve.

BREAD STICKS

Make **one-half Nitty Gritty Bread recipe.** Add with unbleached flour **1 tablespoon garlic oil** and **1 cup grated Cheddar cheese.** When ready for shaping, shape into pencil-thin sticks by rolling between your palms. Roll each stick in **sesame seeds.** Allow to rise for 15 minutes. Bake at 350⁰ for 20 minutes. Yields 4 to 5 dozen.

NITTY GRITTY DOUGHNUTS

Make **one-half Nitty Gritty Bread recipe,** but rather than forming loaves, stretch or cut into doughnut shapes. Fry in hot **oil** until golden on each side. Drain on paper. Shake in paper bag with **brown sugar** and **cinnamon.** Yields about 2 dozen.

GRANDMA'S CABBAGE BUNS

Make **one-half Nitty Gritty Bread recipe.** Any leftover dough may be used for bread or cinnamon rolls if you wish. Yields about 20.

Simmer **1 pound ground beef.** Drain off fat and crumble with a fork. Add **1 head cabbage, chopped,** and **1 large onion, chopped,** and simmer until tender, covered. When done, mix together and add **salt and pepper** to taste.

Pinch off a tennis-ball-size piece of raised dough. Roll out on a floured board into individual rectangle about 3-1/2 by 7 inches. Place 2 or 3 heaping tablespoons of meat and cabbage mixture in the center of one end of the rectangle. Bring one side over to meet the other side and pinch together.

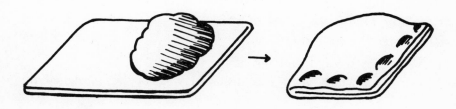

Place buns on greased cookie sheet 2 inches apart. Allow to rise one hour. Then bake in preheated oven set at 350° for 30-40 minutes, or until golden. Eat hot or cold.

NITTY GRITTY CINNAMON ROLLS

Make **one-half Nitty Gritty Bread recipe,** or use any amount of dough left from some other project. Roll out the dough on a floured board or table as thin as you can—no more than 1/4 inch thick. Spread dough with **butter** and **honey.** Sprinkle with **cinnamon, raisins or currants,** and **walnut bits.** Begin rolling wide end of rectangle tightly, rolling toward other side.

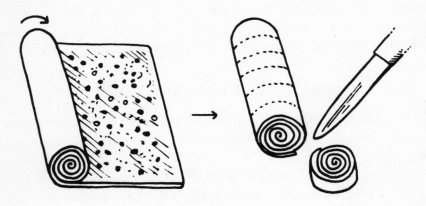

When complete rectangle is rolled, slice into 1-inch-wide slices.

Grease a large baking pan with **butter or margarine.** Spread a layer of **honey or brown sugar** over the butter. Place the rolls, touching, in the pan. Allow to rise one hour. Then bake at 350° until golden, 30 to 45 minutes.

Spread brown paper or towel on table. Turn pan upside down immediately after removing it from the oven. The honey or brown sugar will be syrupy and will coat the rolls. Eat and enjoy!

Common breadmaking mistakes

If the bread doesn't rise:

1. Yeast was too old and not active.
2. Water in which yeast was dissolved was too hot; it killed the yeast.

3. Water in which yeast was dissolved was too cold to activate the yeast.

4. Flour was too coarse; use a finer flour or add more yeast. If the bread caved in, it rose too high in the pan before baking.

If the bread is too crumbly:

1. Dough wasn't moist enough.
2. Dough was kneaded too little.
3. Flour was too coarse.
4. Too much wheat germ was added.

Cornell University did some experiments to improve bread nutritionally so it would be healthfully sustaining. Their results suggest the following changes for any cookie, bread, or cake recipe.

Put in the bottom of each measuring cup of flour:

1 tablespoon soy flour
1 tablespoon milk powder
1 teaspoon wheat germ

The Nitty Gritty Bread recipe takes Cornell's findings into consideration, although the wheat germ was omitted because the flours used were fresh, whole-grain flours. If you do add wheat germ, it is best to get the health-food store variety. The wheat germ found in grocery stores is usually without the wheat germ oil, which contains vitamin E; also, it contains added preservatives.

YEAST

Yeast is a micro-organism that reproduces itself. In former times, yeast was continued by keeping the yeast starter going, and sometimes it was made from hops.

YEAST STARTER

If you are isolated and have only enough yeast for one baking, mix together **yeast** and **water,** as given in directions on yeast package, and **4 cups flour.**

Put one cup of the mixture into a separate container, using the balance for that day's baking.

Set the cup of reserved mixture aside to rise a while, and then put the cup away in a cool place.

The next time you bake, use what you have set aside as your starter in place of yeast, and continue in that fashion. That's what Grandma often did for leavening before the days of readily available packaged yeast.

HOP YEAST

1/2 pound hops
1 gallon water
1 cup fine malt flour
1/2 pound brown sugar

Boil the hops until the water is strong. Then strain and stir in the malt flour. Strain through a coarse cloth. Boil 10 minutes. Cool to lukewarm, and stir in the sugar. Place in a loosely covered jar, keeping it lukewarm. Cover tightly after it has finished working, and keep in a cool place.

UNYEASTED BREADS

Unyeasted breads are simple concentrated goodness, but they require a lot of chewing.

Those interested in macrobiotics feel that some grains are particularly heat-producing and others less so; therefore, some grains are more suited for use in winter and others for use in summer.

Good summer grains are wheat, barley, rye, and corn. Good winter grains are millet and buckwheat. Brown rice can be used any time. It is good to grow accustomed to using a wide variety of grains and flours.

FLOUR TORTILLAS
(the traditional Mexican bread)

Our family prefers the flour tortillas. They are more pliable for use in cooking. However, this same recipe can be used with corn meal to make corn tortillas.

2-1/2 cups unbleached flour
1/2 teaspoon salt
1/3 cup lard
1/3 cup warm water

Mix ingredients together and knead until smooth. Separate into golf-ball-size rounds. Let set covered with a damp cloth for 1/2 hour, then roll into very thin circular cakes. Cook on both sides on an ungreased griddle. When done, they'll have browned spots and still be pliant enough to roll without breaking. Yields about 1 dozen.

Eat tortillas as a substitute for bread, or in combination with other ingredients as one-dish meals.

ENCHILADAS

Fill tortillas with **grated cheese** and **chopped onion.** Roll, top with **chili sauce,** and bake.

Or, more traditionally, cover bottom of cast-iron skillet with **oil.** Add **1 cup water, 1/2 teaspoon salt,** and **3 tablespoons chili powder.** Dip the cooked tortillas in this hot mixture, then fill with grated cheese and onion, and roll. Nest the enchiladas together in the liquid in the skillet and simmer until cheese melts, then turn and simmer until done.

TACOS

Fry tortillas in **oil** until crisp, holding with tongs to create a U shape.

Drain on paper towels and fill with:

lettuce
onion
tomato
browned hamburger

Add **cooked green peas,** if desired. Garnish with **taco sauce.**

For taco chips, fry cut bits of corn tortillas in hot oil until crisp, drain, and serve.

CHAPATTIS
(a traditional bread of India)

These are similar to Mexican tortillas.

2 cups whole-wheat flour
2 tablespoons oil or melted fat
3/4 to 1 cup water
1/2 teaspoon salt

Mix ingredients together and knead until smooth. Roll between hands to create golf-ball-size rounds. Let stand at room temperature an hour or two, covered. Roll into thin, flat cakes and cook on hot griddle until crisp, oiling each side of the chapatti rather than the griddle. Good served with curry. Yields about 10.

SUSAN'S SEASONAL BREADS

Summer	Winter
2 cups whole-wheat flour	2 cups whole-wheat flour
1 cup barley flour	1 cup buckwheat flour
1 cup brown-rice flour	1 cup corn flour
1 tablespoon salt	1 teaspoon salt
2 cups water	2 cups water

Mix dry ingredients together thoroughly, then add the water gradually, stirring well. Knead dough for 5 minutes, until thoroughly pliable. Place in oiled bread pan. Cover with damp cloth. Let rise overnight in a warm place. Bake in 325° oven for 2 to 2-1/2 hours, until done. Yields 1 loaf.

AUNT MARGARET'S CINNAMON CRISPS

These are similar to the crispies that tempt you in bakeries. Combine:

3 cups flour
1 teaspoon cardamom
2 tablespoons brown sugar

Into this mixture cut **1 cup margarine.** Set aside.

Dissolve **1 package or 1 tablespoon yeast** in **1/4 cup warm water.** Blend in:

1/2 cup milk
1 beaten egg
3 teaspoons oil

Stir yeast mixture into flour mixture just until moist. Cover and chill until firm, about 1 hour. Remove dough to floured board and knead four times. Roll into an 11- x 18-inch rectangle. Sprinkle with **cinnamon** and **sugar.** Roll as for cinnamon rolls. Wrap and chill 1 hour. Slice into 1/2-inch slices. Roll each slice into a very thin circle, about 5 inches in diameter. Dredge each with **brown sugar** on both sides. Place close together on ungreased cookie sheet and bake 15 minutes at 350⁰ or until golden. Remove from cookie sheet while warm. Yields about 2 dozen.

Sourdough

Sourdough is a yeasty starter for leavening hotcakes, bread, and also cake. Sourdough is more hearty than yeast, which deactivates in a short time. The combination of wild yeasts in the sourdough starter is tough and adapts somewhat to its environment. For example, in an old house which has accumulated lots of yeast in the air over a period of time, the sourdough will be much more active and even take on some new taste characteristics.

Old sourdough starters have two main origins—the Alaska Gold Rush and the California Gold Rush. Water is the base of the Alaskan starter; milk is the base of the Californian starter.

Old-time prospectors took their sourdough pot to bed with them at night to keep it warm and working. On long, cold journeys, they often wore it, thickened with flour, in a bag around their neck.

Sourdough is a nutritious food, better for you than ordinary hotcakes or bread. During the sourdough process, the sugar and starch are converted to lactic acid, which gives it the sour odor and also creates usable protein.

Soda can be added to the batter just before baking to make the food lighter, but never add it to the starter or it will kill the yeast. Mix sourdough in a glass or pottery container. Never use metal and never leave a metal spoon in the container.

SOURDOUGH STARTER

Mix:

2 cups flour
2 cups warm water
1 packet or cake of yeast

Put 1/2 cup of the mix in a clean jar with a tight cover and the remainder in a covered bowl. This way you won't forget to set aside a half cup as starter for the next time. Put in a warm place overnight. Next day refrigerate the jar of starter. Use the remainder immediately in making pancakes or bread. The starter mixture which has gotten bubbly is called the "sponge."

Use the starter weekly, or "sweeten the pot" by adding **2 cups flour** and **2 cups water.** Let set overnight, then keep all or only the half cup. This is how you sweeten starter that is too sour or make extra for giving away.

Starter will keep quite well for several weeks, although it may separate. If not used sooner, you'd best freeze it or dry it to keep it from spoiling. To transport, either dry it in a flat dish or add enough flour to shape it into a ball and place it in a sack of flour. Water and warmth will activate it.

If your starter turns orange or pink, it's fine—it's just that an odd organism was added. If it turns blue or green, you should throw it out.

My starter is over one hundred years old and originated with the Alaskan Gold Rush. It has never turned an odd color, but it has gotten more sour, and it always separates and looks queer. It creates delicious food, however. I keep a reserve half cup of starter in the freezer so that if I ever forget to set aside the half cup, I won't have lost my starter forever.

SOURDOUGH PANCAKES

Place 1/2 cup starter (see preceding recipe) in a mixing bowl and add 2 cups warm water and 2 cups flour. Beat and set in a warm place overnight. Next morning, set aside 1/2 cup of the "sponge" in the refrigerator for starting the next batch. To remaining sponge add:

1 or 2 eggs
1 teaspoon salt
1 teaspoon soda
1 tablespoon honey

Beat, and then add 2 tablespoons oil. Fry on a hot griddle until brown. Serves 3.

Variation

Add 1/2 cup wheat germ to the batter, using 2 eggs.

WAFFLES

For waffles, make the batter slightly thicker. To the sponge add:

2 eggs
1 teaspoon salt
1 teaspoon soda
2 tablespoons honey

Beat, and then add 4 tablespoons oil.

SOURDOUGH BREAD

Set the sponge, as for Sourdough Pancakes, the night before. Set aside the usual 1/2 cup for next time. Next morning, add to remainder:

4 cups flour
2 tablespoons sugar
1 teaspoon salt
2 tablespoons oil

Mix and knead, adding more flour if necessary. Place in bowl, cover, and let rise until double. Dissolve **1/4 teaspoon soda** in **1 tablespoon warm water** and add to the dough. Knead, shape, place in pans, and let rise. When double, bake at 375° for 50 to 60 minutes. Yields 1 loaf.

SOURDOUGH CAROB OR COCOA CAKE

Mix and let set 2 to 3 hours in a warm place until bubbly:

1/2 cup starter
1 cup water
1-1/2 cups fine flour
1/4 cup dry milk

Cream together:

1 cup brown sugar	**1 teaspoon cinnamon**
1/2 cup shortening	**1-1/2 teaspoons soda**
1/2 teaspoon salt	**6 tablespoons carob or**
1 teaspoon vanilla	**cocoa**

Add **2 eggs** and beat. Combine creamed mixture with sourdough mixture. Mix at low speed until blended. Pour into 2 layer-cake pans or 1 larger pan. Bake at 350° for 25 to 30 minutes.

Milk Variation of Starter

For use with any of the above recipes.

To **1/2 cup starter** add **1 cup flour** and **1 cup water**. Mix, then set aside the half cup starter in a jar for next time. To remainder, add **1 cup flour** and **1 cup milk**.

Let set overnight, and in the morning proceed as usual.

When using the milk variation, be sure to extract the half cup starter for next time *before* adding the milk; otherwise the starter will be permanently altered. The starter should consist of only the initial water, flour, and starter, unless you want to change it.

Pasta

Pasta is a pleasing variation for your diet. But if you're using noodles, macaroni, and spaghetti made from refined white flour and no eggs, you'd better stick with potatoes and brown rice.

TO COOK PASTA PROPERLY

Boil **7 quarts water for each 1 pound pasta.**

Add **2 tablespoons salt** and **1 tablespoon oil** to the boiling water. The oil will help keep the pasta from sticking together and will prevent the pot from boiling over. Cook pasta until soft, stirring frequently. Do not overcook. Fresh pasta cooks much more quickly than dry. If you can't watch it closely, boil for 5 minutes, cover tightly, then turn off the heat. It will finish by itself. This method also works well for keeping the pasta until time for serving.

Note: There are several types of noodle and spaghetti presses. A kind lady has loaned me one that resembles the wringer portion of an old washer. It's fun to use and makes uniform spaghetti and noodles when fed rolled-out, semidry dough. There's another type that you operate by simply pressing the ball of dough through it. (See *Directory of Sources.*)

Nutritious pastas are easy to make at home. You can make a small quantity for one meal or a large quantity to dry and store in jars for later use. Here's how.

EGG PASTA

3 cups fine whole-wheat   or   4 cups semolina flour
  flour   (from Italian food stores)
1 cup unbleached flour
4 beaten eggs
1-1/2 teaspoons salt
2 teaspoons olive oil
2 teaspoons warm water

Mix well until smooth. If the dough is gummy, add a little flour.

Knead. Cover and let set an hour or so. Then roll out on a floured board with a rolling pin or a 2-foot length of broomstick. When semidry, cut into shape desired, or put through a spaghetti or noodle press. Then dry completely, turning occasionally. Before storing, dry at least a day until dough is brittle. Any remaining moisture could cause spoilage. Cook in **boiling water** to which has been added **2 tablespoons salt** and **1 tablespoon oil.**

QUICK EGG NOODLES, OR "FUNNY NOODLES"

If there's no time to roll and dry the pasta, the recipe for **Egg Pasta** also makes a quick egg dumpling. In our family we call these "Funny Noodles" because of their irregular shapes. Kids love to stir these up, shaping them into little balls between their palms.

Make up the dough as directed. After kneading and with no time lapse, simply drop by the spoonful into **boiling soup or water**; cover the kettle until dough is cooked through. For extra fluffiness, add **1 teaspoon baking powder** when mixing dough.

GREEN NOODLES

Here's a sneaky, delicious way to use the excess spinach from the garden.

3/4 pound fresh spinach
3 cups whole-wheat flour
1 cup unbleached flour
2 beaten eggs
1 teaspoon salt

Cook the spinach, drain, and purée; or blenderize raw spinach with the eggs. Then follow the directions given for Egg Pasta.

Variation

You can dry the extra garden spinach for winter use. (See *Drying Foods*.) Use by crumbling fine with a rolling pin. Then, make above recipe substituting **1/2 cup dry spinach** for fresh spinach and **1 beaten egg** for 2 eggs. Add **2 tablespoons water.**

PASTA WITHOUT EGGS

2 cups whole-wheat flour
1 cup unbleached flour
2 tablespoons olive oil
1 teaspoon salt
1 cup warm water

Follow the same directions as for Egg Pasta.

TOMATO SAUCE

8 cups puréed fresh or home-
 canned tomatoes
2 tablespoons olive oil
1 onion, chopped
1 teaspoon fresh milled pepper

1 tablespoon salt
1 clove garlic
1 tablespoon oregano
1 tablespoon basil

Mix and simmer over low heat for 3 or 4 hours. Refrigerate or freeze the extra—it gets better with age.

MY GRANDMA'S GERMAN FRUIT-NOODLE DUMPLINGS

This delicious food is best described as fruit encased in a noodle dough. It has always been served in my family as a main dish on special occasions or in summer when fresh berries are plentiful.

Make the **Egg Pasta dough.** Roll out. When semidry, cut into 4-inch squares. In the center of each square put **2 or 3 tablespoons berries or cherries.** Bring the four corners together in the middle and pinch the edges together tightly. It may help to dampen the edges. Slip each dumpling carefully into boiling water.

While the dumplings are cooking, heat **1 quart milk.** Add **2 or 3 tablespoons browned, melted butter.** When the dumplings are finished, lift them carefully from the pot with a slotted spoon. Set in casserole dish, and top with the warm milk and melted butter. Serve hot, sprinkled with **sugar,** if desired.

If there are leftovers, they'll be great served cold the next day.

When I was growing up, there was always a battle for the leftovers. Very filling!

POTATOES AND PASTA

This dish was traditional with my German immigrant forebears, as it was economical, tasty, and filling.

Make **Egg Pasta,** as above. In a pot of boiling water put **6 diced potatoes.** Spoon Egg Pasta into the boiling water. Cover and simmer until potatoes and irregular noodles are done. Put into a casserole dish with slotted spoon and top with **1 quart warmed milk** and **4 tablespoons browned, melted butter.** Serve hot.

Salads

Salads should provide a kiss of freshness in your daily diet. While I prefer to serve a platter of raw vegetables, whole and sliced, at each meal, I include below some favorite salads. For making any salad of fresh vegetables, follow the directions below.

Wash salad vegetables with cold water only. Never soak them. Drain on a soft cloth or paper towel. Store in a plastic food bag or covered refrigerator dish. When preparing salads, add foods of as many colors as possible. Break vegetables or trim with scissors rather than shredding, when possible. When tossing a salad, the ingredients should be dry. First add the oil, and toss until the leaves glisten with the coating. The oil seals in the taste and locks in vitamins, minerals, and enzymes. And the oil absorbs the seasonings. Toss gently with a wooden spoon and fork, then add remaining ingredients and toss again.

SPRING SALAD

Gather and wash **1 gallon loose, fresh spinach or wild lamb's quarter leaves** (*Chenopodium album*) and **1 cup mushrooms.** (I prefer to use wild edible Oyster Mushrooms in the spring.

However, you should not attempt to gather wild mushrooms until you are very familiar with them. Cultivated mushrooms from the market will be fine.)

Fry **4 slices bacon** until done. Remove bacon and sauté spinach and mushrooms in the grease. Drain. Toss leaves in **a little lemon juice or vinegar.** Garnish with **bacon bits** and **1 or 2 sliced hard-boiled eggs.**

The greens will have cooked down considerably; a bag cooks down to a bowlful. Serves 4.

BULGUR WHEAT SALAD

This salad is a nutritious meal in itself and includes only raw foods.

Soak together overnight **2 cups warm water** and **1 cup bulgur wheat.** Bulgur wheat is cracked, parched whole wheat. If you have no bulgur wheat, you may crack and parch your own wheat. (See instructions on page 103.) Or use soaked whole wheat in the salad, if desired.

Finely chop:

1 medium onion
1 green pepper
3 tomatoes
1 stalk celery

Add **2 cups alfalfa sprouts** and mix all together with drained wheat. (Put any wheat water in your next bread.)
For a meat salad, add **1 cup cooked, chopped chicken or fish.** Garnish with one of the dressings below or with **vinegar and oil,** if desired. Serves 6 to 8.

MAYONNAISE

Place **1 egg yolk** in blender. As blender whizzes, very slowly add **1 cup safflower, sunflower, or soy oil.** Mixture should thicken. If it curdles, add **1 tablespoon hot water.** Then add **2 tablespoons cider vinegar, a dash of salt,** and a **pinch of dry mustard.**

NATURAL FRENCH DRESSING

Use with any salad of fresh spring greens.

Combine in a pint jar with a tight cover:

2/3 cup safflower, sunflower, or soy oil
1/3 cup cider vinegar
1 teaspoon salt

1/4 teaspoon dry mustard
1/2 teaspoon paprika
1 teaspoon tomato juice
1 clove garlic, chopped

Shake to blend, then refrigerate. Shake well before serving. Makes 1 cup.

Russian Dressing Variation

Blend together:

1/2 cup natural French dressing
1/2 cup mayonnaise
1/4 cup chili sauce
1/4 cup cucumbers, chopped
1 hard-cooked egg, chopped

Makes 1-1/2 cups.

Roquefort Cheese Variation

Add to **Natural French Dressing** recipe: **4 tablespoons mashed Roquefort cheese.**

Soups

Soups are a pleasant addition to a meal, whether served hot or cold, in winter or summer.

Soups are a versatile food that usually improves with innovation and experimentation. Below are four basic soups. Feel free to vary the ingredients and create your own. Use what you have, varying quantities to taste.

When making hot vegetable soups, generally begin with the

meat stock, bones, and bone marrow. Miso soy paste adds protein and is a pleasant addition to or substitute for meat. Next, add the onion, garlic, and spices—all but pepper. The vegetables are added during the last hour, and pepper right before serving.

VEGETABLE SOUP

Sauté in a soup pot in a little oil:

2 cups meat, cubed, about 2/3 to 1 pound
1 onion, chopped
2 cloves garlic, chopped

Add:

Marrow from 1 cracked bone
3 quarts liquid (leftover vegetable juices)

Bring to a boil. Then reduce heat. Add:

4 potatoes, cubed
4 carrots, sliced
2 cups cooked beans
3 tablespoons miso soy paste
1 teaspoon chili powder
2 cups celery, chopped,
   or leaves
2 cups tomatoes, fresh
   or canned

2 cups cabbage, chopped
3 bay leaves
1 teaspoon thyme
1 teaspoon basil
1 teaspoon sugar
1 tablespoon salt
1 teaspoon tumeric

Simmer until vegetables and meat are tender, perhaps 40 minutes to an hour. Then add **1 teaspoon black pepper.** Simmer 5 minutes, and serve with fresh baked bread. Serves 4.

CHILE CON CARNE

Sauté in soup pot:

2 pounds ground beef
2 onions, chopped
3 cloves garlic, chopped

Drain fat. Add:

6 cups tomato juice
1/4 cup chili powder,
   or to taste
1 tablespoon salt

1 teaspoon sugar
4 cups tomatoes, fresh
   or canned
2 green peppers, chopped

Simmer as long as possible, the longer the better. One hour before serving, add **4 cups cooked beans,** preferably kidney beans (or add soaked but uncooked dry beans, beginning in the morning and allowing to simmer all day). Right before serving, add **1 cup grated Cheddar** or **Monterey Jack cheese.** Stir and serve. Serves 6.

FRUIT SOUP

Fruit soup is a pleasant variation. My grandmother often serves it on special occasions, especially in late winter or early spring when fruit is a special treat. Although I've usually eaten this soup hot, either as an appetizer or a main dish, it's also delicious as a cold dessert topped with whipped cream and slivered almonds.
   Soak overnight in enough water to cover:

1 pound prunes
1 cup raisins
1 sliced orange
1/4 pound dried apricots, or
   peaches, or pears

1 sliced lemon
1/2 cup sugar
1 stick cinnamon
4 tablespoons tapioca
1 cup dried apples, chopped

Next morning add **more water** to a soupy consistency. Simmer until the fruit is soft, about 1 hour. Then brown **1 tablespoon butter** and **1 tablespoon flour,** stirring and breaking apart. Stir a small amount of soup into butter and flour mixture. Then add to soup. Home-canned or fresh fruit may be used, but add it in the morning. Just remember that dried fruit is concentrated, so increase quantity if using fresh fruit. Serves 6.

BARBARA'S BERRY SOUP

I first experienced this cold soup at a mountain picnic on a hot summer day. It was memorable.

To **2 cups fresh berries, sieved** or **blended,** mix in:

1/2 cup yogurt
1/3 cup sugar
2 cups ice water
1/2 cup red wine (fresh berry wine, if desired)

Cool and serve.

Staple Standbys—Rice, Beans, Lentils, Peas, and Soybeans

In addition to the grains, fruits, and vegetables you keep on hand, you'll want to store a large supply of staple foods for cooking—brown rice, dried beans, lentils, split peas, and soybeans. All are economical and rich in the B vitamins. Served in proper combinations, they are a good source of high-quality protein, although alone they don't contain all the essential amino acids. For example, beans and brown rice served together make a complete protein as do soybeans and sesame seeds.

These dry staples are old stand-bys around the world, in cultures both Eastern and Western. Beans and soybeans are easy to grow in your own garden.

Store staple foods such as these in a tight, dry container. If you live in a geographic area plagued by weevils, several bay leaves placed on top of the food before securing the lid will discourage them. Tape shut any containers of staple foods not to be used for a while and store in a cool, dark, dry place. Staple stand-bys will keep for months, even years this way.

Remember to allow a sufficiently large pot for cooking these dried foods. They will expand two to four times in volume during cooking. A pressure cooker will greatly speed cooking time.

BROWN RICE

I suggest brown rice rather than white because it still has the vitamin-rich outer layer. This layer has been removed in refining white rice. Brown rice may be used in any rice recipe.

BROWN RICE DELUXE

Pressure cook, or bring to a boil **2 cups brown rice,** then simmer in enough water to prevent sticking until tender and somewhat nutty in taste and texture.

Brown on all sides in **vegetable oil** until tender: **1 cup beef, cubed in 1/2-inch pieces, about 1/3 to 1/2 pound.**

Sauté in vegetable oil:

1/2 cup onion, chopped	1 tablespoon soy sauce or
1/2 cup celery, chopped	tamari
1 cup alfalfa sprouts	1/2 cup yogurt or sour
1 teaspoon curry	cream (optional)

Serve meat mixture over the rice. Also good meatless with drained, boiled rice sautéed along with the vegetables. Serves 5.

GREEK-STYLE LENTIL OR GREEN PEA SOUP

Bring **1 quart water** to a boil. Add:

1 cup lentils or green peas	1/2 cup celery, chopped
1 large onion, chopped	1/2 cup carrots, chopped

Simmer 1 hour. Add:

1/2 cup tomato sauce	2 cloves garlic
1 bay leaf	2 tablespoons oil
1 tablespoon parsley flakes	Salt to taste

Simmer until tender, about 1 hour. Before serving, add **a dash fresh ground black pepper** and **1 tablespoon vinegar** (optional) to each bowl. Serves 4 to 6.

BULGUR

Bulgur is parched, cracked whole wheat. It has a sweet, nutlike flavor and cooks faster than unparched wheat. Add cooked bulgur to salads instead of croutons, or use as an extender for meatloaf. Prepare bulgur as follows:

1. Wash the wheat well in cool water until the drained water is clean.
2. Cover with water and boil until liquid is absorbed and kernels are tender and twice their original size, about 35 to 45 minutes.
3. Spread thinly on a cookie sheet and bake in oven at 200° F. until dry.
4. Rub kernels between your hands to remove any hulls or chaff that remain.
5. Use your flour mill set on coarse to crack the bulgur, then store in a tight container.
6. To cook, boil in water for 5 to 10 minutes until double in bulk.

CHEESE AND BULGUR PILAF

In a heavy skillet heat **1/4 cup bacon drippings or oil.** Sauté **1/4 cup chopped mushrooms** and **1 chopped onion** until golden. Add **2 cups bulgur** and **1/2 cup toasted sesame seeds.**

Stir until sesame and bulgur are coated with oil. Then add:

1 clove garlic, minced
1 tablespoon parsley, chopped
1/4 cup celery, chopped, or 2 tablespoons dry celery leaves
1/4 cup carrots, chopped
4 cups miso, chicken, or beef stock
1/2 cup leftover chicken or beef, chopped (optional)

Simmer 15 minutes, then place in a casserole. Sprinkle top with **1/4 cup grated Cheddar cheese.** Brown in oven or broiler and serve hot. Serves 6.

DRIED BEANS

Dried beans should be soaked in water overnight to hasten the cooking. Simply place them in three times their volume of water, such as 1 cup beans in 3 cups water. Next day, bring to a boil, then simmer until tender.

REFRITOS

Bring **1 cup pinto beans** to a boil, then simmer until tender. When tender, mash with a potato masher. Add to taste **chili powder** and **sea salt.** Sauté mixture in a little **vegetable oil** in a heavy skillet. Serve garnished with **grated sharp Cheddar cheese.** Serve with a tossed green salad. Serves 4.

MOM'S BEAN AND RICE DISH

Boil or pressure-cook **1/2 cup brown rice** and **1/2 cup butter beans or large lima beans** until tender.

Brown **8 slices bacon,** cut into 1-inch pieces, and **1/2 cup chopped onion.** Drain grease. Mix together rice, beans, bacon, onion, and add **2 cups condensed tomato soup** (no water added) and **2 tablespoons salad dressing or mayonnaise.**

Put into a casserole, laying two or three strips of bacon across top if desired. Bake at 350° 45 minutes to 1 hour. Delicious hot or cold. A delightful picnic food. Serves 5.

BEAN BURGERS

Combine:

2 cups cooked, puréed red beans	**2/3 cup sunflower seed meal**
1/4 cup onion, chopped	**2 tablespoons sunflower, soy, or safflower oil**
1/2 teaspoon chili powder	
1 teaspoon sea salt	**1/2 cup wheat germ (more**
3 tablespoon catsup	**or less, added as a binder)**

Mix together well and form into patties. Bake 15 to 20 minutes at 350° on an oiled cookie sheet, or broil 5 minutes per side until browned. Place **a slice of cheese** on each burger before serving. Serves 4.

SOYBEANS

Soybeans are a remarkably inexpensive and versatile food. Soy beans are very high in protein; they have a good, but incomplete, concentration of amino acids. Soybeans form a complete protein when used in combination with sesame seeds, wheat, or rice. They may be substituted for beans in any bean recipe to increase the protein and reduce the starch.

Soybeans can be substituted in your diet for vegetables, nuts, dairy products, grain, and meats. Soybeans should be cooked thoroughly before use because raw soybeans contain a factor that inhibits protein utilization.

SOYBEAN SPROUTS
(Vegetable substitute)

Cover soybeans with warm water, and soak overnight. In the morning, drain off water and set on a dark shelf. Rinse daily with fresh water and drain. When sprouts form, place the container in the light for a day or so to green the sprouts. Refrigerate soybean sprouts for several days before eating to improve the nutritional value. (See section on *Seed Sprouting*.)

SOYBEAN FLOUR
(Grain substitute)

Grind soybeans into flour and use for baking, or buy preground soy flour. Untoasted soy flour tastes somewhat bitter, like raw beans. Toasted soy flour (also called soya flour) has an improved, nutlike taste. You can toast your own soybeans or soy flour. However, as soy flour is rich in fat and protein but has little starch and almost no gluten, don't use it to replace more than 2 tablespoons per cup of flour in yeast-bread recipes. Soy flour may be added to meatloaf as an extender.

ROASTED SOYBEANS
(Nut substitute)

Cover **1/2 cup dried soybeans** with **1-1/2 cups warm salted water.** Let soak overnight. Next morning dry the beans on a towel. When fairly dry, put the beans in a heavy, oiled skillet and brown them until golden. Or bake oil-coated beans at 275° until golden. Sprinkle with **onion powder, garlic powder, chili powder, or barbecue powder.**

SOY MILK
(Dairy substitute)

Blend thoroughly **1 quart water** and **1 cup soy flour.** Cook in a double boiler for 20 minutes. Skim off the scum and set it aside to put in bread. Pour the resulting milk in a quart jar, cool, and serve.

SOY CHEESE OR TOFU
(Dairy substitute)

As above, make one recipe of **soy milk.** Remove from the heat and immediately add **4 tablespoons lemon juice** and **3/4 teaspoon sea salt.** Stir once and let cool undisturbed. In 20 minutes the curd will form. Then pour into a cheesecloth placed in a strainer and let set overnight in a sink or basin. Put a weight on top if you want a dry cheese. Refrigerate the next morning. Good with **garlic or onion powder, chili powder, soy sauce,** or the seasoning of your choice. Serve as a spread or as desired. Yields 1 cup.

SOY BALLS
(Meat substitute)

Tastes similar to chicken or veal. Serve with spaghetti sauce or your favorite sauce. Or cook in a soup broth like dumplings.
Mix together:

- **1 cup soy flour**
- **3 tablespoons yeast (a strong-flavored yeast is best)**

Blend together:

- **1 tablespoon sesame, soy, sunflower, or safflower oil**
- **3 tablespoons milk**
- **3 eggs**

Combine mixtures, mixing until smooth. Chill 1 hour or longer. Drop balls of mixture into a pot of **boiling water.** Cover and simmer 10 minutes. Serves 4.

SOYBURGERS
(Meat substitute)

Soak **1 cup soybeans** overnight in **water** to cover. Next morning, simmer beans in the water in which they were soaked, together with the following for 2 hours:

1/8 teaspoon cayenne
1-1/2 teaspoons oregano
1-1/2 teaspoons sea salt
5 cloves garlic, chopped
1/2 cup red wine (optional)

Simmer until thick, then remove from heat and cool immediately. Blend in:

1/2 onion, chopped
2 tablespoons milk
2 eggs

Mold into patties and fry on one side only in an oiled, heavy frying pan until brown. Top with **grated Cheddar or Monterey Jack cheese.** Cover pan and cook burgers 5 to 7 minutes over low heat until cheese melts. Serves 4 or 5.

MISO AND TAMARI
(Flavoring)

Miso and tamari are fermented flavorings made from soybeans. They should be used instead of the common soy sauce, which includes too many adulterants added to simulate fermentation to be healthful. Miso paste can be used, for example, in stew, where it lends the flavor of beef broth. Tamari is a perfect flavoring for plain brown rice and should be used in place of soy sauce. Both are good to flavor gravies or sauces.

GLUTEN
(Meat substitute)

Gluten is a meat substitute that can be made at home from hard winter wheat. Each kernel of wheat contains both starch and protein. These elements can be separated after the wheat is ground into flour. Gluten is a tough, elastic substance containing 57% fiber,

36% protein, and 5% fat. Gluten consists of amino acids from the wheat protein. Wheat gluten is a high-protein food, containing almost three times the protein of beef and six times the protein of whole wheat. Wheat gluten can be stewed in pieces in soup, served sliced like roast or chipped beef, or formed into sausage or hamburger-like shapes. Used with seasoned sauces and in tasty meatloaves, it is difficult to distinguish from meat.

To make gluten, knead together **7 cups wheat flour** and **2 cups cold water.** Knead the dough severely for ten minutes. Beat it, pound it, stretch it—the more, the better. This combines the glutenin and gliadin in the flour into a proper rubber-like consistency.

Now wash away the starch. To do so, cover the dough with cold water and let it stand for an hour. Then work the dough in hot water, hot as your hands can stand. Change water until it is clear. Save the starchy water for a filler in soups and sauces, for thickening gravies, or for breadmaking.

About 1-1/2 cups raw gluten will result. Drain the gluten and knead into a smooth ball. Cook in one of the following ways:

1. Form into sausages, bake and brown.
2. Press into a loaf pan. Bake at 350⁰ for 1 hour. Slice, or cut into cubes for stew.
3. Roll thin and bake on a cookie sheet until brown. Cut into meatlike pieces.

After the gluten has been baked, it should be simmered before serving in order to soften the fiber and to create a more meatlike taste.

NONMEAT PROTEINS

There are many reasons for eating nonmeat sources of protein, such as seeds, grains, and legumes.

One of the most obvious is economy. Seeds, grains, and legumes can provide a nutritious, high-protein family meal for one-fifth to one-tenth the price of meat. However, as the world-wide food crunch escalates, we can expect the price of even nonmeat proteins to rise as demand increases and supply decreases.

Seeds, grains, and legumes pass on to the consumer much less adulterants and poisons—pesticides, hormones, and other additives—than meat. Poisons such as DDT have accumulated in much larger quantities in animals raised for food than in food plants. Some poisons, such as DDT and mercury, accumulate more readily than others. The cycle of fish offers one notorious example. The tiny fish which has accumulated some level of mercury and pesticide poisoning is eaten by a larger fish. This fish accumulates the level of poisoning acquired by all the smaller fish he eats. Then the larger fish is eaten by a still larger fish. When we eat a very large fish, such as a tuna, we are receiving a tremendous accumulation of poisons.

The same kind of thing occurs with red-meat animals, particularly beef cattle. They receive a wide selection of additives in their feed and in other ways—pesticides, antibiotics, hormones. Their pastures may also have been sprayed. So a large amount of poisons accumulates in a small amount of meat. The safest meat to eat is meat you've raised yourself on your own organic pasture.

Another reason for acquiring protein from seeds, legumes, and grains is ecological. We are facing environmental disaster because our energy demands, including food, are greater than our resources.

We face famine on earth because of poor methods of agricultural production, distribution, and consumption. The world population is growing so fast that if it is not controlled, and if our food habits don't change, we will be facing a protein crisis. Currently, this situation exists in many parts of the world where sufficient protein for good health, including vegetable protein, is simply not available.

We have reached a time when we simply cannot afford our current system of meat production—ecologically or economically. We must learn to eat low on the food chain, to eat the protein plants ourselves rather than eating the animals that ate the protein plants in such huge quantities.

The chart below shows how legumes, seeds, grains, and dairy products may be combined to provide complete proteins supplying the essential amino acids. For more information on using vegetable proteins, I suggest you read Frances Moore Lappé's *Diet for a Small Planet* and Ellen Buchman Ewald's *Recipes for a Small Planet.*

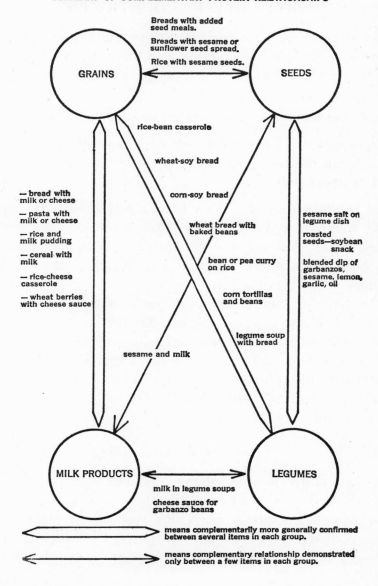

SUMMARY OF COMPLEMENTARY PROTEIN RELATIONSHIPS

Wholesome Desserts

Desserts should be as nutritious as the rest of the meal. Fruit is a fine dessert, and here are others that take a little more effort.

NITTY GRITTY COUNTRY PIE

This delicious pie is economical, yummy, nutritious, and almost a meal in itself. It can be made with any fruit that is available.

Pastry

Blend together with a pastry cutter, or with two knives:

2 cups flour (1 cup whole-wheat, 1 cup unbleached)
2/3 cup shortening or lard
1 teaspoon salt

until kernels the size of peas are formed. Add **about 4 tablespoons cold water,** then knead slightly. (Too much kneading makes a tough crust.) Roll out into 2 crust-size rounds. Put 1 crust in the bottom of a 9-inch pie plate; save the other for covering the filling.

To roll the crust more easily, put a round of dough inside a 12-inch plastic bag and roll out. Or use an oiled paper bag. This trick controls the size and makes clean-up easier. If you don't have a rolling pin, use a wine bottle, empty or filled with cold water and corked. If you don't have a pie plate, use a 2-inch-high, 8-inch cake pan for a deep dish pie. Oil can be used rather than lard, but the crust won't be flaky.

Rhubarb Custard Filling

Rhubarb is free for the gathering in most areas in the spring. Pull the stalks from the ground (they'll grow back), trim the ends, and remove any stringy fibers (the younger the plant, the less stringy the stalk). Cut into 1/2-inch pieces. The following rhubarb filling is much more mellow in taste than most rhubarb pies you've eaten.

Mix together:

3 beaten eggs
3 tablespoons milk
2 cups brown sugar
3/4 teaspoons apple
    pie spice

4 tablespoons tapioca,
    cornstarch, or flour
4 cups rhubarb,
    or 2 cups rhubarb plus
    2 cups cherries

Pour into pastry shell. Dot with **1 tablespoon butter.** Top with the other pastry crust, either whole or cut into a lattice. Bake at 400⁰ for 50 to 60 minutes until brown. Cool until thickened, then eat!

CAROB BROWNIES

Mix **4 beaten eggs** with **2 cups brown sugar.** Add, mixing well:

3/4 cup whole-wheat flour
3/4 cup unbleached flour
1 teaspoon baking powder
1 teaspoon salt

6 tablespoons carob,
    or 3 tablespoons carob
    plus 3 tablespoons
    cocoa
1/3 cup oil

Then add **1 cup sunflower seeds or nuts.**
Spread in a greased and floured 13- x 9-inch pan. Bake at 350⁰ for 35 to 45 minutes until solid. Cut. Firms as it cools.

SOURDOUGH DESSERT OR BRUNCH

Make **Sourdough Pancakes.** Mix together:

2 cups warm water
2 cups flour
1/2 cup sourdough starter

Let set overnight, then refrigerate a half cup of starter mixture for next time. To the remaining **sponge,** add:

1 or 2 eggs
1 teaspoon salt
1 teaspoon soda
1 tablespoon honey

Beat, then add **2 tablespoons oil**. Pour onto a hot, oiled griddle, using 1/2 cup batter for each hotcake, so the diameter is 6 to 8 inches. Spread with **4 tablespoons yogurt** and roll up. Top with **fruit syrup or fruit**, such as **strawberries, maple syrup, or honey**. Superb and delicate. Serves 6.

WALT'S GREAT-GRANDMA'S CHRISTMAS COOKIES

Mix together thoroughly:

1/2 pound almonds, blanched and cut fine	1 teaspoon cardamom, ground fine
1/4 pound citron	1 teaspoon soda in a little sweet milk
4-2/3 cups brown sugar	
3 teaspoons ground cloves	1/2 cup shortening
Rind and juice of 1 lemon and 1 orange	5 beaten eggs
4 tablespoons honey	
4 teaspoons cinnamon	

Work in **8 cups flour (5 cups whole-wheat, 3 cups unbleached)**, a little at a time. Let the dough stand overnight. Then roll out, cut in pieces (any size), and bake in a moderate oven (350° to 375°) until golden brown. Use enough flour to make the dough very stiff. The yield depends on size of pieces, but it makes a very large batch.

HOMEMADE INSTANT COOKIE MIX

Stir up this mix and store in a covered can. Then when you want cookies in a hurry, complete with a variation and bake.

Combine:

2 cups whole-wheat flour	1 teaspoon salt
2 cups unbleached flour	1/2 cup non-fat dry milk
3 teaspoons baking powder	2 cups brown sugar
1/2 teaspoon soda	1 teaspoon cinnamon

With a pastry cutter or two knives, cut in **1-1/2 cups lard** until fine.

This is the basic mix to store for future use. Two cups of the mix makes about 2 dozen cookies. To make plain cookies with the mix, add 3 tablespoons water and combine well. Drop by the spoonful onto a greased cookie sheet. Bake at 400° for 10-12 minutes until golden.

Variations

For **Chocolate Chip Cookies**, to 2 cups of mix add **4 tablespoons water, 1/2 cup chocolate bits, 1/2 cup chopped nuts.**

For **Oatmeal Cookies**, to 2 cups of mix add **1 cup rolled oats, 1 cup raisins, 1 teaspoon vanilla, 1 beaten egg, 1/3 cup water.**

For **Christmas Sugar Cookies**, to 2 cups of mix add **1 teaspoon almond extract, 1 beaten egg, red or green food coloring.** Drop cookies, or roll on floured or sugared board and cut into shapes.

For **Chocolate or Carob Cookies**, to 2 cups of mix add **6 tablespoons cocoa or carob powder, 1 egg, 2 tablespoons milk, 1 teaspoon vanilla, 2 tablespoons peanut butter.**
For **Coconut Almond Cookies**, to 2 cups of mix add **1-1/2 cups coconut, 1 egg, 1 tablespoon milk, 2 teaspoons almond extract.**

For **Pumpkin Sunflower Seed Bar Cookies**, to 2 cups of mix add **1/2 cup cooked pumpkin, 1 teaspoon vanilla, 1 egg, 1 teaspoon cinnamon, 1/2 teaspoon nutmeg, 1/2 teaspoon cloves, 1/4 teaspoon allspice, 1/2 cup sunflower seeds.** Spread on a greased cookie sheet. Bake. Cut into bars.

YUMMY HEALTH BARS

Mix together in blender:

1 cup oil
1 cup honey
1 cup molasses
4 eggs
2 whole oranges, segmented

Combine and blend with liquid in blender:

1 cup whole-wheat flour	1 teaspoon ginger
1 cup soy flour	1-1/2 teaspoons salt
2 cups dry milk powder	1 teaspoon cinnamon

Mix together and fold in:

1/2 pound dried apricots, chopped
1 cup toasted wheat germ
1 cup oatmeal

Bake in a greased and floured 13- x 9-inch pan at 350⁰ for 35 minutes or until firm. Cool and cut into bars.

ICE CREAM

Ice cream is delicious on hot summer days, and also during the winter when snow is available to pack the freezer.

Ice-cream freezers come in two varieties—hand-driven and electric. They work by continually keeping the freezing ice cream mixed and smooth by means of a rotating dasher.

Beat well and put into the freezer can:

4 eggs	1/2 teaspoon salt
2-1/4 cups brown sugar	5 cups milk
4-1/2 teaspoons vanilla	4 cups heavy cream

I substitute 8 cups goat milk for the cream and milk, and it makes a rich ice cream.

For variation, add your choice of one:

1-quart jar home-canned cherries, or
1-quart jar home-canned peaches, puréed, or
   Root beer extract to taste, or
2 cups chocolate chips, or
1 tablespoon black walnut extract

Put the covered can in the freezer and start the dasher. Then put 2 inches of **crushed ice** around the freezer can. Top with **2 tablespoons coarse rock salt.** Continue layering ice and salt

until ice comes up to the edge of the lid of the can. Drain the
brine periodically. When the ice cream begins to firm, yet is still
slightly mushy, the motor will stall or the crank become hard
to turn. This should take 1/2 hour to 1 hour. Stop and remove
the dasher. Cork the lid, and cover the can with ice and more
salt. Insulate with layers of newspaper or a rug. After an hour
or two, the ice cream will be firm. Or remove the can from
the bucket and freeze firm in your freezer. Serve when firm, and
listen to the praise. Serves 4.

Note: A minimum of 1 cup of rock salt will be required for
each batch of ice cream. If you don't use enough, the ice cream
will be very slow to firm and may never firm. If you use too
much salt, the ice cream will freeze too rapidly and become coarse
instead of smooth.

A hand-driven freezer works well, especially if you can recruit
crankers. If you have surplus milk and would like to make ice
cream frequently, an electric ice-cream freezer is worthwhile.

HONEY-BAKED APPLES

Wash and core **apples** (1 per person). Set in baking dish. Spoon
2 tablespoons honey on each apple. Sprinkle with **cinnamon.** Cover
and bake at 325° until soft, about 25 minutes.

AMBROSIA

Agar-agar is a sea plant which comes packaged in little crystalline
blocks from health-food stores. Use it instead of gelatin. Soak **2
blocks agar-agar** in a little cold water until soft.

Mix **1 cup dried fruit (your choice), 3 cups water,** and **3
cups apple juice** and bring to a boil. Then add the **softened
agar** and boil for 15 minutes. Add **apple pie spice or nutmeg,
cloves and cinnamon,** and refrigerate until jelled. Agar-agar is
very high in vitamin A and iodine, and is a good substitute for
commercial gelatin desserts, which contain lots of white sugar and
chemicals. Serves 4.

Beverages

Beverages are very important in the maintenance of good health. Yet most of us drink too little liquid, and the type of liquid we select is usually the poorest quality from a nutritional standpoint. We need one to two quarts of liquid a day.

Perhaps the most important beverage, and the most ignored, is water. Nothing can compare with the goodness of fresh water. Our mountain spring water is pure, tastes good, and is full of natural minerals.

The ideal is to have a fine, pure artesian well, but if you don't, or if you live in a city where tap water is your main water source, I suggest bottled water, free of chemical additives. It should not be distilled though, as we do need the minerals. In our fancy, complex society, you may have to develop a taste for plain water. Most people are habituated to coffee or carbonated beverages. Try a glass of cold water in place of these, and you'll soon discover water is a superb refreshment.

Fruit and vegetable drinks are very enjoyable, and you can make them at home. Vegetable juices will generally require a juicer—an expensive investment.

Fruit can be squeezed through a sieve or puréed in a blender, then strained if desired, to obtain the juice.

All juices are best fresh. Fruit and vegetable juices are rich in vitamins A and C. It's best to eat your fruits and vegetables whole most of the time, however, as the nutrients and bulk of the pulp are good, too. If you do use a juicer, make the pulp into a sandwich spread.

Basket of Fruit

GRAPE JUICE

Fill clean, quart canning jars half full of **grapes**. Add **2/3 cup sugar** per jar. Fill jars with **boiling water** to within 1/2 inch of the top. Cover each with a canning lid and ring. Process in a boiling water bath 15 minutes. Tighten lids to seal.

HOT MULLED CIDER

Most people don't have access to a cider press, so you'll probably have to buy the cider.
  Combine in a pan:

  1 gallon apple cider
  1/4 cup honey
  Juice of 1/4 lemon
  2 tablespoons whole cloves
  1 cinnamon stick

Simmer slowly for 15 to 20 minutes. Serve hot. Serves 12.

QUICK CITRUS COOLER

Squeeze into a tall glass the **juice of 1/2 lemon** and the **juice of 1/2 orange or lime**. Fill glass with ice cubes. Fill with cold water. Sweeten to taste. Garnish with lemon slice. Very refreshing.

HOMEMADE TOMATO JUICE COCKTAIL

Simmer **tomatoes** (10 pounds makes approximately 3 quarts of juice), then use a sieve to separate juice. Fill quart canning jars with **tomato juice**. To each jar, add:

  1 teaspoon celery salt
  1 tablespoon lemon juice
  1/2 teaspoon onion juice
  1 drop Tabasco sauce

  Couple drops Worcester-
    shire sauce
  1/4 teaspoon sugar

Cover jars with canning lids and process in boiling water bath for 15 minutes. Tighten lids. If preferred, use finely grated celery and onion to taste, omitting celery salt and onion juice and adding plain salt.

MILK

Milk is rich in vitamins A, B, and D, and is a complete protein. Milk as a beverage is very filling and sustaining.

EGG NOG

Blend together in blender:

3 eggs
3 cups whole milk
2 tablespoons brown sugar
2 teaspoons vanilla
A pinch of salt

If beating by hand, beat egg whites first, then yolks, then add other ingredients. Sprinkle with **nutmeg to taste.** Serves 8.

QUICK MILK COOLER

Blend together in blender:

1 cup milk
1 piece fruit (peach, banana, or 1/2 cup berries)
1/2 teaspoon vanilla
2 ice cubes

Sweeten to taste and serve. Also try **1/2 banana** and **1/2 orange** together.

COLLEEN'S HOMEMADE INSTANT COCOA MIX

A quick wintertime treat. Delicious and much cheaper than purchased mix. I only regret that you must purchase the ingredients. Shake together in a double grocery bag:

1 8-quart box dry powdered milk
1 1-pound box instant cocoa mix (like Quik)
6 ounces instant coffee creamer
1/2—1-1/2 cups powdered sugar

Put 1/4 to 1/3 cup of mixture into a mug. Fill with boiling water. Stir and serve. Makes about 50 servings.

COFFEE SUBSTITUTES

In place of coffee, so full of caffeine, I suggest you try Yannoh, a healthful coffee substitute. Yannoh is made from barley, wheat, soya, chickpeas, rice, dandelion, and burdock roots. You prepare this aromatic brew the same as ordinary coffee. Yannoh is available at health-food stores.

Substitute coffees were popular during the Depression, when the cost of regular coffee was prohibitive. Make your own. Makes about 40 servings.

ERSATZ COFFEE

Mix together **8 cups wheat bran** and **2 cups corn meal.** Beat in **3 beaten eggs** and **1 cup sorghum molasses.** Spread on cookie sheet and dry in oven at 200° to 225°. Stir frequently while browning. A handful serves 2. Sounds odd, but it works.

TEAS

Black and green teas are much better for you than high-caffeine coffee, but herb teas are vastly superior to ordinary teas. Furthermore, not only is there a wide, tasty variety of herb teas, but some have high vitamin content, and others are claimed to have medicinal value.

Some of the more common sources of tea which can be gathered are mint, rose hips, spruce and pine needles, and strawberry leaves. Spruce and pine needles contain more vitamin C than a comparable weight in oranges; rose hips contain considerably more. Rose hips are the little red berries left on the bushes after the roses have bloomed. They are gathered from wild roses in the fall. Wild mint and strawberry leaves are gathered in spring and summer, sorted, air-dried, then brewed.

To brew tea

Fill teapot with hot water and let stand 10 minutes. Pour out. Then place leaves and flowers of the desired herb or herbs into the pot. Cover with boiling water. Put the lid on, and allow to steep 10 to 15 minutes, preferably covered with an English tea cozy or with the pot wrapped in a towel. Serve with honey.

Most roots and barks must be simmered 1/2 hour. The maximum goodness can be extracted from herbs by steeping 24 hours. This works especially well for a tea that's to be served cold.

Make your own tea mixtures. For example, to a good imported black tea, add dried orange peel and cloves. Or add mint and rose hips. If you sweeten, use honey.

SUN-BREWED ICED TEA

Fill a half-gallon bottle with **water**. Drop in **3 rose hips tea bags** and **3 spearmint tea bags.** Hold paper tabs outside jar by screwing down the lid over the tea-bag strings. Set jar in sun from morning till evening, then set jar in refrigerator overnight. Delicious no-effort iced tea will be awaiting you the next day. Add ice cubes if desired. Works with most teas, herbs, and combinations.

MRS. SHETH'S GINGER TEA

4 teaspoons powdered ginger
1 teaspoon powdered cinnamon
1/2 teaspoon powdered clove
1 teaspoon powdered black pepper
1/4 teaspoon powdered cardamom

Mix together and store in a bottle. Then use a pinch or two to flavor regular black tea. Delicious with milk added. This has been one of my favorite teas since it was served to me by friends who had recently arrived from India.

Frivolities

Most of these "frivolities" have little or no nutritional value. But most people occasionally have a frivolity anyway.

CHERRY CORDIAL

Fill a quart jar with **cherries.** Add inexpensive **vodka** to within 2 inches of the top. Add **1 cup sugar.** Put a lid on loosely, allowing room for expansion and for the air to escape. Store in a cool place. Every couple of weeks open the lid to let out the air, and add whatever sugar the liquid will absorb. The cordial will be ready in three or four months, in time for Christmas if you make it at harvest. Serve the clear liqueur in glasses. Use the alcoholic cherries as a sauce for ice cream, if you wish. I prefer to liquefy the entire contents in the blender. This makes a thick, tasty, opaque liqueur. Try it both ways.

WINE

Fill a jar or other container two-thirds full of **cherries** or fruits such as **apricots or peaches.** Add **1 cup honey or sugar** and cover lightly. Later add more sugar and water to taste, but always allow room in the jar for expansion. If you don't, the top is likely to blow off under the pressure of fermentation. One way to avoid this is to rubber-band a balloon to the top. This keeps away insects, but allows space for expansion.

The mashed fruit will settle to the bottom, and you can siphon off the clear liquid with a thin, flexible tube, like aquarium tubing. Or strain it through several layers of cheesecloth. Be sure to strain when finished, however, or the wine will turn to vinegar—high-quality vinegar, but vinegar nevertheless. Be sure the wine has stopped "working" before bottling. One year the tops blew off some of mine after they were bottled as gifts!

Grapes

MARIGOLD OR DANDELION WINE

On a sunny day, pick: **4 quarts marigold flowers** or **2 quarts dandelion flowers.** Pick only the petals, no green parts or stems. Wash them in cold water. Place blossoms in a large glass bowl or earthenware crock. Top with **1 grated lemon** and **1 grated orange.** Cover with **1 gallon boiling water.** Cover the bowl and let it set for 4 days for marigolds or 10 days for dandelions. Strain the liquid into a saucepan and heat it to the boiling point. Then pour it over **3 pounds granulated sugar** in a bowl. Stir until the sugar is dissolved. When it cools to lukewarm, add **1/4 ounce yeast for marigolds** or **1/2 ounce yeast for dandelions.** Cover the bowl and set aside for 3 days, stirring daily. Strain again, then bottle, covering loosely at first. Refill any bottles that lose liquid. After a while, when the wine has quit "working," cap tightly. It will be ready to drink in 6 months, if you can wait that long. Yields 1 gallon.

MEAD

Bring to a rolling boil **1 gallon water** and **5 pounds honey.** Simmer, skimming periodically. Remove from flame, stir, and skim off the scum. The scum is the residual beeswax, and should be removed. Pour into a crock. Add the **juice of 2 lemons** and the **peel of 1 lemon.** Add **4 cloves, 1/2 ounce ginger root,** and **2 sprigs rosemary, well-bruised.** When at wrist temperature, add **1 ounce powdered yeast** and cover lightly. Remove the lemon peel after 3 days. After 6 days, skim, strain into bottles, and cork or cap lightly. After 6 weeks, tighten the seals and store the bottles on their sides in a cool place. Gets better the longer it ages. Yields 1 gallon.

POTATO CANDY

Peel and boil **1 large white potato.** Mash, then add **a pinch of salt** and **confectioner's sugar** (as much as you can work in). Roll out the resulting stiff dough. Spread it with **peanut butter, honey, or jam.** Roll dough up like a cinnamon roll, then refrigerate until cool and firm. Slice into bite-sized pieces and serve.

SNOW TAFFY

Choose a patch of **clean white snow.** (Yellow or gray snow won't do.) Heat to 250°:

   1 cup brown sugar
   1/3 cup water
   1/3 cup light corn syrup
   1 teaspoon salt
   1/4 cup butter

Then add **1 teaspoon vanilla** and pour over the snow.

SNOW ICE CREAM

Dissolve **1 cup brown sugar** in **1-1/2 cups milk.** Flavor and color with **a little cherry or berry juice.** Stir in enough **dry, powdery, clean snow** to make a thick consistency. Serve.

CARAMEL CANDY OR TOPPING

Good any time, but best of all, keep on hand for a wintery weekend. Place **1 can sweetened condensed milk** unopened in a pan. Cover with water. Boil slowly for 3 hours, making sure the can is covered with water at all times (so it won't explode from pressure imbalance). Then open the can, cooling it first, if you desire. You will find inside a rich caramel candy. For a thick topping for rice pudding, custard, or ice cream, boil in the can 2 hours. For a chewier caramel, boil 4 hours. Sweet and easy.

PUMPKIN BRANDY

Wash and dry **1 large pumpkin.** Cut off the top and take out the seeds. Set them aside to roast. Put in the pumpkin's cavity **14 cups brown sugar, 4-1/2 cups raisins,** and **2 cakes yeast.** Put top back on the pumpkin. Set pumpkin in a pan. Let mixture work until pumpkin's pulp dissolves. Strain. Allow yeast to settle, then strain again through several layers of cheesecloth. Bottle. Make sure it has stopped fermenting before capping tightly. Makes about 2-1/2 quarts.

Baby Food

Many adults have grown accustomed to preparing healthful organic foods for themselves, yet continue to cheat baby. They feed baby with canned foods and formulas loaded with white sugar, salt, and chemicals. Read those labels. Babies should eat even better than adults, since they are forming the bodies and habits that will go with them through life.

Breast feed your baby if you can. If you can't, or don't wish to, don't hassle yourself. Just try to prepare a healthful formula using fresh milk (preferably goat's milk), water, and honey in the proportions and according to the directions suggested by your doctor, Dr. Spock, or Adelle Davis. Keep in mind that honey

and dark corn syrup will loosen baby's bowels; light corn syrup will firm them. Adjust the formula accordingly.

There are other reasons besides good nutrition for preparing baby's food yourself. One is economy. Baby can dine well on the family's leftovers. One puréed carrot serves as baby's vegetable dish, yet might otherwise be wasted. One carrot might equal one jar of baby food—minus the water, cereal, seasonings, and chemicals. Besides, the food you prepare has more nutrients—it hasn't been highly processed. You know what you're feeding. Freshness is important, too.

For baby cereal, simply grind whole grain fine—probably rice or wheat when you first begin feeding solid foods. Cook in a little water. Or purchase whole-grain flour and mix with a little warm water to serve as a cereal. If you sweeten, use honey or molasses. But, as you're tempted to add sugar and salt, remember your tastes for these have been acquired; baby doesn't have them and may be best left without. A little apple juice or warm milk is good stirred into the cereal.

Avoid baby-food juices. Serve instead the finest unsweetened regular juices you can buy. It's better—and much cheaper, besides. When baby is ready for applesauce, buy a regular can or, better still, make your own.

When family leftovers are too sizeable for one baby meal, purée foods alone or in combination and freeze in small jars or in ice-cube trays. If you freeze foods in ice-cube trays, after they are frozen remove them from tray, package, and label.

If baby spits bland vegetables, *don't* add salt or sugar—simply mix in a little fruit or fruit juice.

A blender is very worthwhile for making baby food—it pays for itself quickly. A pressure cooker helps in cooking food to an extremely soft consistency. A Happy Baby Food Grinder costs little and is convenient to carry along, takes up little space, and makes baby food on the spot. (See *Directory of Sources.*)

BANANA YOGURT

Here's a quick baby food—delicious, and easy on the tummy, too. Blend together **1 cup yogurt** and **1 banana.**

As soon as your baby can pick up objects and move them in the direction of his or her mouth, it's time to begin finger foods, important for coordination, sensory experience, and independence.

ZWIEBACK

Cut **homemade whole-grain bread** in 1/2- x 1-1/2-inch pieces. Spread on a cookie sheet and bake at 250⁰ until dried out, about 1 hour.

TEETHERS

Blend together:

- 1 teaspoon vanilla
- 2 tablespoons molasses
- 2 tablespoons honey
- 2 tablespoons oil
- 1 egg yolk

Add:

- 1 tablespoon soy flour
- 1 tablespoon wheat germ
- 1-1/2 tablespoons dry powdered milk
- 3/4 cup whole-wheat flour

Mix well, then roll out on ungreased cookie sheet no more than 1/4 inch thick. Cut into pieces about the size of baby's fingers. Bake at 350° for 15 minutes. Remove from sheet and cool thoroughly, then store in jar. Yields several dozen.

As baby gets teeth, grows into a toddler, and graduates from baby foods, be sure he still eats healthfully. Keep finger foods handy for him, such as carrot sticks, bananas, dried fruit and fresh fruit slices, hard-boiled eggs, boned strips of meat or poultry, and whole-grain biscuits. Make fruit popsicles in summer. Baby will grow healthfully and happily, and hopefully without desire for the chemical feast.

INFANT NUTRITION

Following are daily nutritional requirements for infants:

- *Proteins.* . The amount supplied by 1-1/2 to 2 ounces of whole milk per pound of body weight of the infant.
- *Carbohydrates.* The amount supplied by the above quantity of milk, with an additional ounce of honey or corn syrup for each 10 ounces of milk used.
- *Fats.* As supplied by the milk.

● *Total Fluids.* About 2-1/2 ounces per pound of body weight are needed. The formula is diluted with water accordingly.

●*Vitamins and Minerals.* As supplied by mother's milk. Pasteurized milk is deficient in iron and vitamin C, which calls for early introduction to other foods. Unless the milk is specially fortified (most evaporated milk is), additional vitamin D is also required.

Wholesome Snacks

SESAME CRISP

Measure **1 cup honey.** Work in **sesame seeds** until the mixture is very stiff, and you can't work in any more seeds. Then flatten on brown or waxed paper sprinkled with **fine whole-grain flour.** (Rice flour works well.) Sprinkle more fine flour over the flattened mixture to prevent stickiness. Cover with waxed paper and roll very thin with a rolling pin. Remove the cover and let stand until hardened, or dry in oven at 225° until solid. Cut in squares, and continue drying until crisp.

PEANUT-BUTTER DRY-MILK CANDY

This candy doesn't need cooking, and children love it.
Mix together in a bowl:

1 cup peanut butter
2 cups dry powdered milk
1/2 cup honey

Add the honey a little at a time until mixture sticks together. Shape into little balls. Roll in **fine flour or powdered sugar,** put on a plate, and refrigerate until firm. These candies are rich in calcium and protein.

SNACK MIX

Prepare a cannister of **mixed raw nuts, roasted seeds** and **soybeans, raisins,** and **chopped dry fruits.** Keep your snack dish filled.

FROZEN FRUIT POPS

Purée **1 cup fruit,** or **mixed fruit,** with **1 cup water.**
Pour into ice-cube tray, sticking a wooden spoon in each section.
Freeze. Makes a cooler for big kids and little kids on a hot day.

Variation

Mix **1 can frozen fruit juice** with **1 cup water.** Freeze.

Always keep fresh vegetable sticks and fruit on hand for snacks. If you have a cool storage place and a large family buy fresh fruit by the case. Kids will learn to love wholesome organic snacks if they are readily available. My kids love to eat a tomato, carrot, orange, or peach, or even suck a lemon, after school. Keep peanut butter and apple butter with whole-grain bread handy, too.

PRESERVING AND STORING

Stocking Up

Throughout history humans have learned to store food, to stock up for periods of shortages caused by nature or by man, as a hedge against a poor crop, or to carry the family through until the next harvest.

Methods of preserving and storing food are a venerable art. I've always felt it a good idea to store food reserves for the family. These stores have carried my family through unexpected flood, excessive company, and periods of poverty.

Today most of our society depends on supermarkets and other shops for daily supplies. How fragile are these means of distribution! Our society is so interdependent that one break in the link of the distribution chain could create discomfort or hardship. Few of our cities are well-prepared for any disruption, unlike even the huge cities of China—Peking and Shanghai—whose perimeters grow food sufficient to provide for the inhabitants. Because we are so dependent on transportation to provide supplies, we are vulnerable not only to natural forces like droughts and sudden disasters, but also to strikes, to political upheavals, to economic dislocation, and to transport interruptions of various kinds. Following the famine and starvation experienced by the Mormon people in the nineteenth century, that group has sought to help each member store a year's supply of food at all times. You might wish to follow their example, particularly if you are responsible for children or other adults.

In *The Alice B. Toklas Cook Book,* Toklas writes about the shortages experienced by Gertrude Stein and herself during Hitler's occupation of France in World War II. We do not often think of being hungry and of the difficulties in obtaining food if the system breaks down, so her description is most interesting; although she writes of wartime, similar circumstances could result from other causes. I refer you to her chapter "Food in the Bugey During the Occupation":

> "In the beginning, like camels, we lived on our past. We had been well-nourished. . . . Requisitioning continued and before the autumn of 1940 any supplies that were not on the coupons were no longer to be found. The grocery stores were empty but before this had happened I had bought dried fruits, chicory to replace coffee, sardines, spices, cornmeal and cleaning materials. The autumn harvest in the vegetable garden would largely see us through the winter with the string beans and tomatoes I had put up. . . . Our vegetable garden had been the prettiest one for miles about. I was very proud of it and what it had produced. The hard work had exhausted me. Suddenly we realized that we were hungry but it was not mentioned. It was at this time that I dreamed one night of a long silver dish floating in the air and on it were three large slices of succulent ham. That was all. It haunted me for the six months that were to pass before the blessed black market was organized."*

Stein and Toklas had been accustomed to affluence; it is interesting to read about how they learned to deal with hardship.

In addition to the food-preservation methods which follow, I have included below charts that will enable you to determine the food requirements for a given number of individuals for a given period of time.

To organize a simple food-storage system, I would suggest buying several cans of food rather than buying one—and setting the extras

*Alice B. Toklas, *The Alice B. Toklas Cook Book* (Anchor Books, 1954), pp. 215, 218.

aside. Or, each week, plan to buy one case of some canned food item, in addition to your regular shopping list. In this way, a considerable supply will gradually accumulate. Dried foods and grains are the simplest to store, and dried grains can be sprouted to provide daily green vegetables. (See section on *Seed Sprouting*.) Dried foods take less space and keep longer than any other. You might wish to put aside some cooking oil, honey, tea, nuts and soybeans for protein, dry powdered milk, seeds for sprouting, dry beans, and dry fruit. These foods alone can provide quite a good diet, if need be. Rotate and replace stored foods to assure freshness. With garden seed and a patch of ground, fresh food can be grown during summer. And for more information, do get a copy of the government pamphlet *Family Food Stockpile for Survival.*

If you are interested in storing just a few foods for survival in an emergency, four long-term, inexpensive keepers are wheat, dry powdered milk, honey, and salt. The wheat can be used not only for baking and for cereal, but also for sprouting and for high-protein gluten meat-substitute. The dry powdered milk is high in protein. The honey is for seasoning and food energy, and the salt in small quantities is necessary for proper bodily functioning and for seasoning. One month's supply of these foods for one adult would include 27 pounds of wheat, 5 pounds of powdered dry milk, 3 pounds of honey, and less than 1 pound of salt.

The chart on page 135 gives the approximate yield per bushel of fruits and vegetables. These are average weights, as the legal weight of a bushel of fruit or vegetables varies in different states.

Food	Fresh	Canned
Fruit		
Apples	1 bu. (48 lbs.)	16 to 20 qts.
Apricots	1 bu. (50 lbs.)	20 to 24 qts.
Berries, except strawberries	24-qt. crate	12 to 18 qts.
Cherries, as picked	1 bu. (56 lbs.)	22 to 32 qts.
Peaches	1 bu. (48 lbs.)	18 to 24 qts.
Pears	1 bu. (50 lbs.)	20 to 25 qts.
Plums	1 bu. (56 lbs.)	24 to 30 qts.
Strawberries	24-qt. crate	12 to 16 qts.
Vegetables		
Asparagus	1 bu. (45 lbs.)	11 qts.
Beans, lima, in pods	1 bu. (32 lbs.)	6 to 8 qts.
Beans, snap	1 bu. (30 lbs.)	15 to 20 qts.
Beets, without tops	1 bu. (52 lbs.)	17 to 20 qts.
Carrots, without tops	1 bu. (50 lbs.)	16 to 20 qts.
Corn, sweet, in husks	1 bu. (35 lbs.)	8 to 9 qts.
Okra	1 bu. (26 lbs.)	17 qts.
Peas, green, in pods	1 bu. (30 lbs.)	12 to 15 qts.
Pumpkin	50 lbs.	15 qts.
Spinach	1 bu. (18 lbs.)	6 to 9 qts.
Squash, summer	1 bu. (40 lbs.)	16 to 20 qts.
Sweet Potatoes	1 bu. (55 lbs.)	18 to 22 qts.
Tomatoes	1 bu. (53 lbs.)	15 to 20 qts.

SOURCE: Bulletin No. AIS-64, *U.S. Department of Agriculture.*

The chart on page 136 is based on the United States Department of Agriculture's *Daily Food Guide.* Only foods that can be canned are listed. Adjust amounts to your family's needs. Plan to can for one year's food supply. Storage amounts for some of the home-canned foods listed here are given for only 36 weeks. The presumption is that you will obtain or grow fresh foods for the 16 weeks of summer. When planning a year's food supplies to be grown or purchased, this chart could be supplemented by the one on the top of page 137.

The list at the bottom of page 137 comprises a group of foods that can be stored for long periods of time. The foods, unsupplemented by other food items, would provide a diet during emergency.

Product	Number of Times Served	Approximate Size Serving	Amount Needed per Person	Amount Needed Family of 4
Citrus fruit and tomatoes (includes juices)	7 per week—36 weeks	1 cup	63 qts.	252 qts.
Dark green and yellow vegetables Broccoli, spinach, and other greens, carrots, pumpkin, sweet potatoes, yellow winter squash	4 per week—36 weeks	1/2 cup	18 qts.	72 qts.
Other fruits and vegetables Apples, apricots, peaches, pears, asparagus, green beans, lima beans, corn, green peas, summer squash, etc.	17 per week—36 weeks	1/2 cup	76 qts.	304 qts.
Meats, poultry, sea foods	4 per week—36 weeks	1/2 cup (2-3 ozs.)	18 qts. or 36 pts.	72 qts. or 144 pts.
Soups	2 per week—36 weeks	1 cup	18 qts.	72 qts.
Jams, jellies, preserves	6 per week—52 weeks	2 tbs.	40 1/2-pts.	160 1/2-pts.
Relishes	3 per week—52 weeks	1 tb.	5 pts.	20 pts.
Pickles, vegetable	2 per week—52 weeks		13 pts.	52 pts.
Pickles, fruit	2 per week—52 weeks		13 qts.	52 qts.

SOURCE: *Ball Blue Book.* Muncie, Ind.: Ball Brothers Co., 1969.

Food	Per week (52 Weeks)	Year (1 Adult)	Year (Family of 4)
Milk (fresh or dry-powdered)	7 pts.	182 qts.	728 qts.
Eggs	1/2 doz.	26 doz.	104 doz.
Flour, cereals, rice, grains	3-1/2 lbs.	182 lbs.	728 lbs.
Split peas, lentils, dry beans, rice, nuts	1-1/2 lbs.	78 lbs.	312 lbs.
Honey, syrup, molasses	1 lb.	52 lbs.	208 lbs.
Fats and oils	1-1/4 lb.	65 lbs.	260 lbs.

Food	1-Month Requirements per Adult	Storage Time*
Wheat, whole-kernel, winter	15 lbs.	indefinite
Mung beans for sprouting	1 lb.	indefinite
Milk, powdered nonfat dry	6 lbs.	indefinite
Sugar, granulated	1 lb.	indefinite
Molasses, blackstrap	1/2 lb.	indefinite
Honey, raw, unadulterated	2 lbs.	indefinite
Shortening or vegetable oil	1 lb.	two years
Peas, dry split and lentils	2 lbs.	indefinite
Beans, dry	5 lbs.	indefinite
Rice, preferably brown	2 lbs.	indefinite
Raisins and other dry fruits	2 lbs.	two years
Salt, iodized	1/4 to 1/2 lb.	indefinite
Baking powder	1/4 lb.	two years
Baking soda	1/4 lb.	indefinite
Dry yeast (can be used as ongoing starter if necessary)	1/4 lb.	6 months at 70° F.

*The storage time given presumes that you have carefully followed directions for storage, and that foods are kept in watertight, vermin-proof sealed containers in a dark place at 40°.
For emergency storage, you might wish to add to one-per-person-per-day supplies 50 mg. vitamin C tablets and multivitamins.

Freezing Foods

Freezing foods for storage is very simple. The advantages of freezing foods are its simplicity, the low cost of supplies, and the good nutritive quality of frozen foods. The chief disadvantage of freezing is its dependence on electricity; if your power goes off for several days, you may lose a year's supply of food. That happened to me when my food freezer burned out over the holidays. Once was enough, and I don't depend so much on frozen food storage anymore. Also, 8 to 12 months is generally the maximum keeping time for frozen foods; canned or dried foods can be stored much longer.

SUPPLIES

You will need:

● Plastic bags and wire or rubber closures. (Plastic containers and glass jars can be used.)
● Paring knife for cutting food.
● Wire basket for blanching. (A blancher is handy.)
● Ascorbic acid or lemon juice to prevent discoloring of fruits.

METHOD

Blanching is needed to stop enzymatic action which will break down the frozen food. Blanch all fruit for a minute or two in boiling water, then plunge into ice water. The skins will come right off. Pour a solution of ascorbic acid or lemon juice over the fruit to prevent discoloration. Berries can be frozen without blanching.

For vegetables, blanch, then cool immediately. Green peppers and tomatoes don't need to be blanched, but may be frozen after washing.

Meats, fish, and poultry should be rinsed (not soaked) in cold water. Bone them to save freezer space. They don't need to be blanched. Double wrap them, first in plastic wrap, then in freezer paper, and freeze immediately.

All packaging should be tight to exclude as much air as possible. Package in the size containers you find convenient. Label and date the containers. Freeze as quickly as possible by spreading containers loosely on the freezer shelf. Pile packages more closely after they're frozen solid.

Canning Foods

"Eat what you can, and what you can't, can," said Gertrude Stein. That's good advice for gardeners and harvest-time bargain hunters alike.

Home canning allows you to keep foods a considerable length of time without special storage conditions. Home-canned fruits, vegetables, meats, jams, and pickles may be kept several years if sealed properly. There will be a slight deterioration of texture and nutritional value the longer they are kept. Home-canned foods keep stable longest if stored in a cool, dry, dark place.

SUPPLIES

Prepare for home canning by acquiring the following:

● Jars and tops. Secure sufficient screw-top jars of standard narrow and wide-mouth sizes. Buy enough flat lids for the jars needed, and two dozen screw-top rings of each size. (Each jar needs a new lid, but the rings can be reused.) Lids, rings, and jars can be purchased at most grocery stores. Secure your supply in June or July, before the rush. Save by buying your jars at rummage sales. Mayonnaise jars are standard size and will work fine; however, the standard canning jar with the brand written on the side is made of heavier glass and will not break as easily. Select pints or quarts according to the size of your family. Odd-sized jars can

MAIN TYPES OF CLOSURES AND HOW TO USE THEM

When canning.—Fit wet rubber ring down on jar shoulder, but don't stretch more than necessary. Fill jar; wipe the rubber ring and the jar rim clean. Then screw cap down firmly and turn it back ¼ inch.

After canning.—As soon as you take jar from canner, screw cap down tight, to complete seal.

Porcelain-lined zinc cap with shoulder rubber ring, to fit standard mason jar.

When canning.—Fit wet rubber ring on ledge at top of empty jar. Fill jar; wipe rubber ring and jar rim clean. Put on glass lid. Push long wire over top of lid, so it fits into groove. Leave short wire up.

After canning.—As soon as you take jar from canner, push short wire down, to complete seal.

Wire-bail type jar with glass lid and rubber ring.

When canning.—Fill jar; wipe rim clean. Fit wet rubber ring on glass lid. Put lid on jar, rubber side down. Screw band on until it is almost tight. Then turn back almost a quarter turn, but be sure jar and band mesh. Caution: If band is screwed too tight, jar may break.

After canning.—As soon as you take jar from canner, screw band down tight, to complete seal.

Glass lid and top-seal rubber ring, with metal screw band, to fit standard mason jar.

When canning.—Fill jar; wipe rim clean. Put lid on with sealing compound next to glass. Screw metal band down tight by hand. When band is screwed firmly, this lid has enough give to let air escape during processing.

After canning.—This is a self-sealing type. Do not tighten screw band further after taking jar from canner.

Flat metal lid with sealing compound, with metal screw band, to fit standard mason jar.

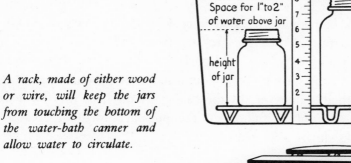

A rack, made of either wood or wire, will keep the jars from touching the bottom of the water-bath canner and allow water to circulate.

be used for jams and jellies. Chipped or cracked jars will not work for home canning. When your jars are empty, store them covered with old lids to keep them clean and unchipped.

● Canners. Secure a water-bath canner for canning fruits, tomatoes, and pickles. Get a pressure canner—more expensive, but essential for canning—for vegetables and meats. Save money by buying your canners at rummage sales. Both kinds of canners should be equipped with racks. The pressure canner should have a pressure gauge and steam-release valve. It should also have a rubber ring, easily replaced if worn.

● Wide-mouth funnel.

● Measuring cup.

● Wire basket or blancher for scalding fruit.

● Ladle.

● Hot pads.

● A small, clean cloth for wiping tops of filled jars.

● A towel.

● A paring knife and a dinner knife.

METHODS

There are two standard methods for canning foods: the cold-pack method and the hot-pack method. In the cold-pack method, raw food is packed in the jars, then the jars are covered and processed. In the hot-pack method, the food is cooked and the jars and tops are boiled separately; then the jars are filled and sealed.

I suggest using only the cold-pack (raw) method. It's easier and less mess, and proper sealing is almost foolproof, unlike the hot-pack method. However, in the raw-pack method, the finished jars of food are not as full as in the hot-pack method, because the food cooks down after packing.

Cold-pack or raw-pack method for high-acid foods (fruits, tomatoes, rhubarb, sauerkraut, and pickles)

Fruits and vegetables may be packed in a syrup or juice containing sugar or salt. However, if you wish to avoid excess salt or sugar in your diet, plain water serves as well. If you do wish to use salt or sugar, they season better if added before canning rather than before serving.

Wash and sort the fruit or tomatoes. The food may be canned skinned or unskinned. If desired, blanch a minute or two in boiling water and plunge into cold water to loosen the skins. Pit, slice, and pack into the clean jars. (Here's where a dishwasher is very handy.) Pack fruit firmly without squeezing; pack tomatoes in more tightly because their shrinkage is greater and they'll be mushy anyway.

If a syrup is desired, fill jars with a solution of **1 cup honey, or 2 cups sugar,** and **6 cups water.**

Tomatoes will create sufficient juice to cover themselves; add a little water if necessary and a teaspoon of salt to each jar if desired.

Run a dinner knife between the fruit and the jar to release any trapped air. Wipe the top of each jar to remove any pulp or seeds that would prevent a seal. Put on the sealing lid, then screw the ring on firmly, but without forcing.

Put the jars in the water-bath canner. Fill the canner with water the same temperature as the jars. The water should cover the jar tops by 2 inches, with another 2 inches allowed as space for the water to boil rapidly. If there's a big difference in the temperature of the jars and the water, the jars will break. Processing time begins when the water boils. Add 1 minute to the time per each 1,000 feet above sea level. See charts for times.

After processing, remove jars from the canner and allow to cool in a draft-free place. Jars are sealed when their lids snap into a concave position. Sealed lids ring if tapped with a spoon. If jars are not sealed, remove the lids to find out why—a bit of fruit between the jar and lid, a faulty lid, a screw ring not tightened, a chipped or cracked jar. Any unsealed jars of food should be reprocessed or refrigerated and eaten.

If you've worked carefully, all the jars should seal. Don't be impatient; jars seal as they cool. Next morning remove the screw rings and store the jars in a cool, dry, dark cupboard. The lids provide the seal; the screw rings only temporarily hold the lids in place.

When serving, do not use any jars of food where the seal has broken.

APPLESAUCE

Wash and sort whole **apples**, cutting out any bad spots. Simmer in a covered pot in a little water. Simmer slowly all day, or overnight if you wish, making sure there is sufficient liquid to prevent scorching. Then force the apples through a ricer or sieve. Save the juice for jelly. Add to the **sieved apple pulp** (to taste) **apple pie spice, or cinnamon and nutmeg,** and **honey or brown sugar.**

Put applesauce in jars and process 10 minutes, plus any altitude adjustment. Store sealed jars when cool. (Although the applesauce is packed in the jars while hot, follow the cold-pack method.)

Processing Time for High-Acid Foods

| Fruits | Type Pack | Water-Bath (212° F.) Processing Time in Minutes | | |
		1/2 Pints	Pints	1-1/2 Pints and Quarts
Apples	Hot	15	20	20
Applesauce	Hot	15	20	20
Apricots	Cold	20	25	30
Apricots	Hot	15	20	25
Berries	Cold	10	15	20
Berries	Hot	10	10	15
Cherries	Cold	15	20	25
Cherries	Hot	10	10	15
Currants	See Berries			
Dried Fruits	Cold	10	15	20
Figs	Hot	80	85	90
Grapes, ripe	Cold	10	15	20
Grapes, unripe	Cold	15	20	25
Grapefruit	Cold	10	10	10
Guavas	Hot	10	15	20
Loquats	Hot	10	15	20
Mixed Fruits	Hot	15	20	25
Nectarines	See Apricots			
Peaches	Cold	20	25	30
Peaches	Hot	15	20	25
Pears	Hot	15	20	25
Persimmons	Hot	10	15	20
Pineapple	Hot	10	15	20
Plums	Hot	15	20	25
Acid vegetables				
Rhubarb	Hot	10	10	10
Sauerkraut	Cold	25	30	30
Tomatoes	Cold	30	35	45
Tomatoes	Hot	10	10	15
Tomato Juice	Hot	10	10	15

SOURCE: *Ball Blue Book.* Muncie, Ind.: Ball Brothers Co., 1969

Cold-pack method for low-acid foods (vegetables and meats)
Home canning is an extremely satisfying art. There are those afraid
to try it because they've heard of danger. There *is* danger from
incorrect procedure, particularly in canning low-acid foods. And
this danger exists equally in manufactured canned foods. This is
the primary reason entire brands of specific products are recalled
from the grocery shelves—and not always before they have reached
the consumer. To me, one of the greatest benefits of home canning
is that I know exactly what I put into the jars, and I know
exactly how the jars of food are processed.

Method
Warning! You *must* follow these directions exactly. Eating
improperly canned vegetables, meats, fish, poultry, or any other
low-acid food may cause botulism, which is usually fatal. The
same danger exists for both home-canned and manufacturer-canned
low-acid foods. You can be sure of the safety of your home-canned
foods by following directions carefully and by using a pressure
canner for low-acid foods.

The use of hot peppers or spices will not prevent this danger.
Throw away any moldy or discolored jars of food or food with
a bad odor. However, the presence of the botulinus microorganism
causes *no change* in the smell, appearance, or taste of food, so
never taste low-acid foods before heating.

The botulinus microorganism is more difficult to control than
most bacteria. It is anaerobic (grows only in the absence of air),
so your vacuum-sealed jar full of low-acid food is an ideal environment for it. Follow the directions below, and as a precaution,
boil all low-acid foods in an open pan 15 minutes before eating.

Processing Times for Low-Acid Foods

Low-acid vegetables	Type Pack	Steam-Pressure Canner (240° F.) 10 Pounds Pressure Processing Time in Minutes	
		1/2 Pints and Pints	1-1/2 Pints and Quarts
Asparagus	Hot or Cold	25	30
Beans, green, snap, wax	Hot or Cold	20	25
Beans, lima, butter	Hot or Cold	40	50
Beets	Hot	30	35
Broccoli	Hot	30	35
Brussels sprouts	Hot	30	35
Cabbage	Hot	30	35
Carrots	Hot or Cold	25	30
Cauliflower	Hot	30	35
Celery	Hot	30	35
Corn, whole-kernel	Hot or Cold	55	85
Corn, cream-style	Hot	85	Not recommended
Eggplant	Hot	30	40
Greens, all kinds	Hot	70	90
Hominy	Hot	60	70
Mixed vegetables	Hot	Length of time needed for vegetables requiring longest processing time	
Mushrooms	Hot	30	Not recommended
Okra	Hot	25	40
Parsnips	Hot	30	35
Peas, black-eyed, crowder, field	Hot or Cold	35	40
Peas, green, "English"	Hot or Cold	40	40
Peppers, green	Hot	35	Not recommended
Potatoes, white	Hot	30	40
Potatoes, sweet	Hot and Dry	65	95
Potatoes, sweet	Hot and Wet	55	90
Pumpkin	Hot	65	80
Rutabagas	Hot	30	35
Salsify or Oyster Plant	Hot	25	35
Spinach	Hot	70	90
Squash, summer	Hot	30	40
Squash, winter	Hot	65	80
Tomatoes, stewed	Hot	15	20
Turnips	Hot	30	35

(Continued)

Meats, poultry, sea foods

Chili	Hot	75	90
Chopped meat—beef, veal, lamb, mutton, pork, chevron, venison	Hot	75	90
Corned beef	Hot	75	90
Cracklings	Cold	50	60
Goulash, meat sauce, stew	Hot	60	75
Ham	Cold	50	60
Headcheese	Hot	75	90
Pork sausage	Hot	75	90
Pork tenderloin	Hot or Cold	75	90
Roasts—beef, veal, lamb, mutton, pork, chevron, venison	Hot	75	90
Spareribs	Hot	75	90
Steaks and chops—beef, veal, lamb, mutton, pork, chevron, venison	Hot or Cold	75	90
Poultry, rabbit, and squirrel —boned	Hot	75	90
Poultry and rabbit—on bone	Hot or Cold	65	75
Chicken à la King	Hot	65	75
Roast poultry	Hot	65	75
Clams		70	Not recommended
Crab meat		100 at 5 lbs.	Not recommended
Mackerel, trout, salmon, shad, etc.		100	Not recommended
Shrimp		45	Not recommended
Smelt (in tomato sauce)		50	60

Soups

Bean or split pea	Hot	50	60
Chicken	Hot	30	45
Clam chowder and fish chowder	Hot	100	Not recommended
Tomato	Hot	20	30
Vegetable	Hot	Length of time needed for vegetable requiring longest processing time	

SOURCE: *Ball Blue Book.* Muncie, Ind.: Ball Brothers Co., 1969.

Carrots

Turnips

Wash the food. Cut into desired size and pack into jars. Cover with water, sauce, or gravy. Add 1 teaspoon salt, and spice and onions if desired. Wipe tops of jars, put on lids and screw rings firmly.

Set jars in the pressure canner. Add 1 inch of water to the canner. Put the lid on tightly. Turn the heat up. After steam has exhausted for 10 minutes, close the petcock (screw knob on pressure-canner lid). The pressure gauge will begin to rise. When it reaches the desired pressure, start timing and turn down the heat so the pressure remains constant. Ten pounds of pressure is required at sea level; add 1 pound per 2,000 feet altitude.

After the required time, remove the canner from the heat. When the pressure has returned to zero by itself, open the petcock and exhaust any steam. Then remove canner lid, lifting the side away from your face so the steam doesn't burn you.

Remove the jars and let them cool. They'll bubble for some time. After they are cool, test seal and store. Reprocess or use any unsealed food immediately. Boil food 15 minutes in an open pan before serving.

Some older canning books will give directions for canning low-acid foods by methods other than pressure canning. They are all risky. There is even more danger at higher altitudes where the boiling point is lower and insufficient for sterilization.

PRESSURE CANNER CARE

Your pressure canner should be examined annually to be sure the rubber ring and the pressure gauge are in good shape. Used canners may need either or both replaced. Canners made during World War II don't have a rubber gasket; they seal by tightening down heavy screws. Your County Extension Agent will either test your pressure gauge or tell you who can. If your gauge works, but is slightly off at each pressure, figure the difference and adjust for it each time. Good hardware stores carry a selection of gaskets and pressure gauges. Presto, National, and Ward's canners are all made by the same company. Order parts from a Ward's catalog store or write National Presto Industries, Eau Claire, Wisconsin 54701.

A regular-size pressure cooker can be used for pressuring pints. Use it at normal pressure for the recommended processing time, plus 20 minutes.

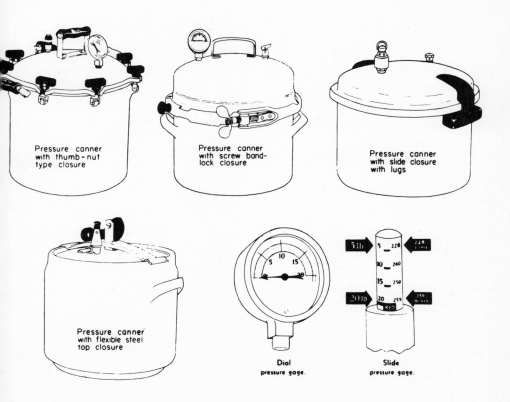

Pressure canner with thumb-nut type closure

Pressure canner with screw band-lock closure

Pressure canner with slide closure with lugs

Pressure canner with flexible steel top closure

Dial
pressure gage.

Slide
pressure gage.

ALTITUDE ADJUSTMENTS

Water-Bath Method: Add 1 minute per 1,000 feet above sea level.

Altitude Correction Table—Boiling-Water Bath Method

Elevation	Boiling Point of Water	Time Less than 20 Minutes	Time Greater than 20 Minutes
Sea level	212.0° F.	Add 0 minutes	Add 0 minutes
1,000 ft.	210.2	1	2
2,000	208.4	2	4
3,000	206.6	3	6
4,000	205.2	4	8
5,000	203.4	5	10
6,000	201.6	6	12
7,000	199.9	7	14
8,000	198.3	8	16
9,000	196.5	9	18
10,000	194.7	10	20

SOURCE: "Canning Colorado Fruit," Bulletin No. 435-A, *Colorado State University, Cooperative Extension Service.*

Pressure Canner: Add 1 pound per 2,000 feet altitude.

Ten pounds of pressure at sea level give a temperature of 240° F. inside the pressure cooker. At higher altitudes an increase in pressure (gauge reading) is necessary in order to reach this same interior temperature. The rule is: For each 1,000 feet above sea level, add 1/2 pound of pressure. This means that at 2,000 feet altitude it takes 11 pounds of pressure to make the internal temperature reach 240° F.

If your altitude is:	Pressure required for 240° F. is:
Sea level	10 lbs.
2,000 ft.	11
3,000	11.5
4,000	12
5,000	12.5
6,000	13
7,000	13.5
8,000	14
9,000	14.5
10,000	15

SOURCE: "Canning Vegetables," Bulletin No. 449-A, *Colorado State University, Cooperative Extension Service.*

Jams and Preserves

Jams and jellies are fruits or fruit juices preserved in sugar or honey. Jellies are made from fruit juices; jams are made from crushed fruit. I usually make more jams than jellies because I don't want to waste the fruit pulp. I make jellies when I have leftover juice, like the juice left after making applesauce.

Conserves are made from a mixture of fruits, often including raisins, nuts, and citrus fruits. Marmalade has small bits of fruit, often citrus fruit, throughout. Preserves are whole fruits or large pieces of fruit in a thick syrup, usually slightly jelled.

ESSENTIAL INGREDIENTS

• *Fruit.* Gives characteristic flavor and furnishes part of the required pectin and acid.
• *Pectin.* Required for jelling the fruit. Some fruits, particularly apples and quinces, have sufficient natural pectin. Underripe fruits have less natural pectin than ripe fruits. Commercial fruit pectins are made from apples or citrus fruit. Powdered pectin is added before heating; liquid pectin is added after boiling. Packaged pectin comes with a number of recipes.
• *Acid.* Needed for flavor and gel formation. The acid content varies in different fruits and is higher in underripe fruits. Lemon juice or citric acid must be added when fruits are low in acid. If acid is lacking, add 1 tablespoon lemon juice to each cup fruit juice. One-eighth teaspoon ascorbic acid powder may be substituted for each tablespoon of lemon juice.
• *Sugar.* Helps in jelling, serves as preserving agent, and adds to flavor. Most jelly recipes call for granulated sugar. Honey can replace up to one half the sugar when no added pectin is used. When making jelly with added pectin in large recipes, 2 cups of honey can replace 2 cups of sugar; in smaller recipes use no more than 1 cup honey as a substitute for proper jelling. However, using honey has no nutritional benefit in jellymaking, as the high heat required is damaging.

Juices from the following fruits are high in pectin content and will readily convert into jelly: green apples, crabapples, unripe grapes, blackberries, currants, gooseberries, raspberries (slightly underripe), cranberries, huckleberries, quinces, and plums.

Pectin and/or acid must be added in making jellies from the following: strawberries, peaches, pineapples, cherries, rhubarb, pears, and sweet apples.

Apples may be added to other fruits to add natural pectin. The following table shows the proportions of sugar and fruit juice to use.

Pectin test

If commercial pectin is unavailable, you may wish to determine the pectin content of your fruit before proceeding. The following methods may be used:

1. Add 1 teaspoon of grain or denatured alcohol (poisonous), 95% strength, to 1 tablespoon fruit juice. Shake and observe; or,
2. To 2 tablespoons juice, add 2 tablespoons sugar and 1 tablespoon Epsom salts. Shake thoroughly, wait 20 minutes, and observe.

In either of the above methods, judge the results in the following way: If a solid mass results, a large amount of pectin is present. In this case, add 3/4 to 1 cup of sugar to each cup of juice. If only slight coagulation occurs, a small amount of pectin is present. In this case, use only 1/2 to 3/4 cup for each cup of juice.

HONEY JAM

Crush **cooked fruit** by putting it through a sieve or ricer, or uncooked in a blender. Stir in **warm, light honey** until fruit is well-covered and yet honey is not excessive. Refrigerate if possible; however, honey is an excellent preservative, so refrigeration is probably not necessary. This recipe preserves all the goodness of the fruit and honey. Just remember, too much honey will cover the delicate flavor of the fruit. The flavor of light honey is more delicate than that of dark.

Bee Hive

APPLE JELLY WITHOUT PECTIN

Select **3 pounds apples** (about 1/4 must be underripe). Wash, remove stems, and cut into pieces; don't peel or core them. Place in a pan, adding **3 cups water.** Cover and bring to a boil. Then simmer for 1/2 hour. Pour into a jelly bag or old pillowcase and let the juice drip. (If you press it, the juice will become cloudy from added pulp.) Strain juice through two layers of cheesecloth to assure clarity.

Measure into a large pan **4 cups apple juice, 3 cups sugar,** and **2 tablespoons lemon juice.** Stir to dissolve sugar. Place on high heat and boil to 8° above boiling point of water. (For proper jelling, test the boiling temperature of water at your altitude that day, as it varies with the weather.) Remove from the heat and skim off foam. Pour immediately into hot containers to within 1/2 inch of the tops. Cover with 1/8 inch hot paraffin, rotating the jars to spread the wax. After that layer of paraffin cools, add a thicker layer of paraffin, not quite so hot.

Or pour into small, hot canning jars. Add a lid and firmly screw down the ring. Turn upside down for 15 minutes, then invert and lid will seal. Cool, label, and date. Store in a cool, dry, dark place. Yields about 4 cups.

SPICED PEACH JAM WITH PECTIN

Scald, skin, pit, and cut **2 dozen medium peaches.** Mash with a potato masher. Measure **3-3/4 cups crushed peaches** into a large kettle. Add **1 package powdered pectin** and **1/4 cup lemon juice.** Stir well to dissolve. Place on high heat and, stirring constantly, bring to a full boil. Stir in **5 cups sugar, or 3 cups honey.** Continue stirring and heat to a full boil. Boil for 1 minute at sea level, longer at higher altitudes, until temperature reaches 8° above local boiling point, or until jam sheets off spoon or coagulates on a cold plate. Remove jam from heat, skim, and stir for 5 minutes. Pour into hot jars to within 1/2 inch of top. Cover with 1/8 inch hot paraffin, adding another layer of paraffin when the first cools. Or, follow sealing technique in previous recipe. Cool, then store.

ORANGE MARMALADE

Slice into small pieces, including pulp and skin, **6 oranges** and **3 lemons.** Set overnight in **10 cups cold water.** Next morning, simmer mixture until fruit is tender and thickened. Measure and add **sugar** (same amount as mixture) and **1 cup chopped walnuts.** Cook until 8° above local boiling point. Pour into jars and seal.

Good marmalades can be made using a mixture of citrus fruits, rhubarb, peaches, etc. Simply measure chopped fruit, soak overnight in three times the amount of water, cook the next day, and add 3/4 cup sugar per each cup of fruit mixture.

WATERMELON RIND PRESERVES

Remove the dark outer peel from the watermelon rind. Cut **8 cups watermelon rind** into 1-inch pieces. Soak overnight in a brine of **1 cup pickling salt** and **1 gallon cold water.** Next morning, drain and soak in clear water for 1-1/2 hours. Drain and repeat clear water soaking. Drain.

Into each pint jar put:

1 maraschino cherry
1 cinnamon stick
1 slice of lemon or orange
1 teaspoon whole cloves
1 teaspoon whole allspice

Cover with a hot syrup consisting of:

8 cups sugar
4 cups water
maraschino cherry juice

Cover with lids and screw tops. Process 20 minutes at sea level, longer at higher altitudes. Store when cooled and sealed. Yields about 8 cups.

Pickling

Pickling is done in open crocks or in sealed jars, usually with a solution of water, salt, and vinegar. Almost any food can be pickled. Pickling has been a traditional method of food storage for hundreds of years. Raw vegetable leftovers may go into a pickled relish.

For fermenting or brining, use a crock or stone jar, unchipped enamel-lined pan, glass jar, bowl, or casserole. Do not use copper, brass, galvanized, or iron utensils for heating pickling liquids. For a lid, use a plate or glass lid weighted down with a jar of water. Or use a double plastic bag filled with sufficient water to force the bag to the sides of the crock to hold the pickles down.

ESSENTIAL INGREDIENTS

● *Fruits and vegetables.* Select tender vegetables and firm fruits. Garden-fresh food is best; brine cannot penetrate the wax-treated food often found at the supermarket counter. Carefully wash all food in cold water before beginning.

● *Salt.* Use pure granulated salt or pickling salt. Uniodized table salt can be used, but chemicals added to prevent caking will cloud the brine. Iodized table salt will darken the pickles.

● *Vinegar.* Use a high-grade cider or white distilled vinegar of 4%-6% acidity (40-60 grain).

● *Sugar.* Use either white granulated or brown.

Poor quality pickles result from the following:

● *Shriveled pickles.* Vinegar, sugar, or salt solution is too strong or the pickles have been overprocessed.

● *Hollow pickles.* Cucumbers are poorly developed or too old; fermentation too rapid; brine too strong or too weak during fermentation.

● *Soft or slippery pickles.* Caused by microbial action resulting from too little salt or acid; cucumbers not covered with brine during fermentation; scum left in the brine during fermentation; insufficient heat treatment; a broken seal; moldy garlic or spices; blossom ends of the cucumbers not removed.

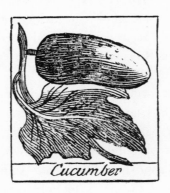

Cucumber

DILL PICKLES

Wash **fresh cucumbers** and soak overnight in a brine of **3/4 cup pickling salt** and **1 gallon water.** Next morning sort according to size. Cut off the blossom end to remove an enzyme that promotes spoilage.

Put into the bottom of each of the required jars:

3 heads of dill
3 bruised cloves garlic
Pinch of alum
Pinch of tumeric (optional)
2 hot chilies (optional)

Pack the small cucumbers whole into the jars. Cut the large cucumbers into sticks or slices and pack. Fill the jars to the neck with a boiled mixture of:

1 quart vinegar
3 quarts water
3 cups pickling salt

Screw lids firmly on jars. Process in boiling water bath for 20 minutes at sea level, longer at higher altitudes. When cool, check seal and store. They're best if aged at least a month or two.

SPICED PEACHES OR BEETS

Into quart jars put **peaches or beets, peeled** (1 peck or 8 quarts). Into each jar, put:

3 whole nutmegs
1 teaspoon whole cloves
1 teaspoon whole allspice
1 cinnamon stick

Make a solution of **11 cups sugar** and **2 quarts vinegar.** Pour over food in jars. Wipe rims of jars and firmly cover with lids and bands. Process in boiling water bath 20 minutes at sea level, longer at higher altitudes. Yields about 8 quarts.

UNSALTED SAUERKRAUT

Into a gallon crock or jar shred **1 large head of cabbage.** Add **bruised dill, celery,** and **caraway seeds.** Pour **cold water** over the mixture until it is covered. Cover with a weighted plate or water-filled plastic bag to hold the cabbage under water. Leave a little space at the top of the crock for fermentation. Cover with a clean cloth and store in a warm room. Daily skim off any scum and make sure the cabbage stays submerged. In about a week it will be ready.

If served fresh, this unsalted sauerkraut is very rich in vitamin C and lactic acid. If desired, process in quart jars for 20 minutes at sea level and store.

DILL CROCK

Into a gallon crock or jar, place:

A layer of dill
A few hot red peppers
1 whole bud of garlic
Another layer of dill
A few grape leaves (if you have them)

Then add any vegetable or mixture of vegetables you wish:

cucumbers	mushrooms
carrots	green tomatoes, or
cauliflower	anything else you
green beans	care to try
onions	
zucchini	

Cover with **another layer of dill.**
Add a boiled brine of:

1/2 cup vinegar
1 cup pickling salt
10 cups water

Be sure the vegetables are submerged in the brine by a weighted plate. Cover with a clean cloth. Set the crock in a cool place. The goodies in the crock will bubble and ferment. Skim off the scum as required. Let the vegetables pickle a week or two before serving.

Serve the vegetable as appetizers or snacks, as desired.

HAMBURGER RELISH

Grind through a food grinder, set on medium setting:

10 large cucumbers, peeled
5 large onions
3 green peppers
3 red peppers

Mix together well. Then pack firmly into clean pint jars. Cover with a brine of:

1 cup vinegar
3 cups water
3/4 cup pickling salt

Cover jars with lids and rings, being sure to wipe food from rims of jars. Process in a boiling water bath 15 minutes at sea level, or longer at higher altitudes. Makes about 10 pints.

Drying Foods

Drying foods is my favorite method of preserving. Nearly anything edible can be preserved by drying. Drying has several major advantages:

1. Little need for special equipment.
2. Little storage space required.
3. No salt or sugar needed to be added.
4. Food can be kept for long periods without refrigeration. (In fact, dried food is frequently found in fair condition in ancient tombs.)

Throughout history man has dried foods when plentiful to assure a quantity and variety of food in lean times. Dried foods are easy to store because they have little weight, take up little space, and remain stable under conditions that would spoil other foods, such as power failures and periods of extreme heat and cold. Moisture and insects are the main enemies of dried foods, but these are avoided by keeping dried foods in a tight container in a dark, dry place.

Food is dried by promoting conditions that remove the natural moisture faster than decaying bacteria can work. Drying is speeded by heat, low humidity, and salt. All three work by drawing moisture from the food.

HERBS

An old-fashioned screened porch is one of the best places to dry foods. When using the oven for drying, make sure to prop it open a crack with a spoon handle, thus allowing moisture to escape.

Gather the herbs, putting any poor-quality sprigs aside for the compost heap. Wash the better sprigs in cool water, then drain in a colander.

I dry my herbs by placing them loosely in an empty net grapefruit bag. Hang the bag in the warmest and driest corner of the kitchen. For the first few days, shake and invert the tied bag several times a day so that all pieces are frequently exposed to the air. When they begin to feel dry, shake the bag only infrequently. When the herbs become dry enough to crumble, store them in tightly closed jars or plastic bags.

The label can be removed from net fruit bags by soaking in warm water. Keep in mind that the dye will bleed.

Other ways to dry herbs include tying the washed sprigs in a bundle.

VEGETABLES

Many vegetables can be strung on a string to dry if the individual pieces are thin enough. Put a knot between two pieces to keep them apart. An example is green beans, strung and called "Little Britches" by the pioneers. The Little Britches are soaked overnight to rehydrate and are excellent served in white sauce.

Mushrooms and peppers can be dried in this way with strings going from beam to beam in the kitchen. You can dry leafy vegetables in net bags. I dry celery leaves for soups and stuffings in bags. All of the above can also be dried on screens. To dry most effectively, the thickness of the vegetable should be less than 1/4 inch. If thicker, it may be best to hang in the sun or dry in the oven at 170°. However, dried foods taste best if kept out of intense heat or direct sunlight.

FRUITS

I have been most successful drying fruits on screens outdoors or in the oven. Small fruits like apricots and plums can be dried in halves, but larger fruits like apples and peaches must be dried in slices. For a fine flavor, better color, and best keeping, dip each piece in honey kept hot in a double boiler. Then place the pieces, not touching each other, on screens in the sun, covered with a cheesecloth or sheet. They must be brought in at night because of dew or if a rainstorm threatens. Most fruit is thick and moist, so oven drying works well. Begin with fruit in a 190° oven for 6 hours, then reduce heat to 170° for 1 day, and then to 140° until fruit is dry enough so that moisture can't be squeezed out, yet is still pliable. (This is my procedure in the mountains, but lower altitudes may require lower heats and moister climates may require longer drying periods.) Allow to "season" an additional day or two in a closed paper bag before storing in plastic bags or jars. This way, remaining moisture will distribute itself evenly among the pieces of fruit, and excess moisture will have a chance to evaporate.

Obtain old window screens discarded in back alleys when affluent folks get aluminum combination windows. Screens can be stacked to save space, or a frame can be built to hold them, much like the rack shown in the section on *Mushroom Growing*. Allow air to circulate freely between the screens. If the screens are loosened from their frames, bind them by lacing with heavy cord.

FRUIT LEATHER

Fruit leather is a fast, efficient way to dry fruit. Pit the fruit and cut out any bad spots. Purée in blender. Then spread about 1/4 inch thick on greased cookie sheets or waxed paper. Dry in indirect sunlight or in oven set at 170° for 24 hours, then reduce to 140°. When dry yet pliable, roll up the sheet of fruit and store in jars or in tightly rolled wax paper. Fruit leather is excellent to take on hikes. It also works well in baking. Simply spread a sheet over a 1/4-inch-thick rectangle of sweet dough, spread with honey and cinnamon if desired, and then bake. Follow instructions for Cinnamon Rolls.

MEATS AND FISH

Thinly slice the meat or fish. Rub the slices with smoke salt, purchased at a supermarket or meat market. If you wish, sprinkle on some pepper for flavoring and to keep flies away if drying outside. Dry in the sun. Spread on screens or hang on the clothesline. Meats and fish may also be dried in the oven. Just be sure to slice about 1/4 inch thick and keep heat at 190° to 200° until drying is well under way. Make sure no two surfaces of the meat touch.

The meat or fish can also be soaked in brine before drying; brine will discolor meat, but not fish. The salt acts as a preservative.

GRAINS

Most grains dry on their stalks before they are harvested. After threshing or winnowing, they are stored in airtight containers.

Grains provide their own individual airtight cases and will stay fresh for a long time if unground. After all, much of our flour is made from grains kept in government or other storage for years. To store grain as airtight as possible, fill the containers to the top. Place lids on tightly, and tape to seal.

Other Storage Methods

Freezing, canning, drying, pickling, and preserving aren't the only methods of storage.

Meats can be smoked and cured for keeping, but still require storage in a cool, dark place, like a basement or cellar.

IN LARD

One old and simple method to keep meat is to cook the meat as you would for the table. Render the lard and bone the meat. Put a layer of meat in a stone crock. Pour some hot, melted, rendered lard over it, completely covering the layer. Continue layering in this way, then cover the top with a layer of lard. Each layer of lard must completely cover and seal the meat. Store in a cool place, at a temperature that allows the lard to remain firm. A cool cellar or basement is fine. Remove the meat as needed. Keeps for some time.

SALTING

Meats can be salted for long-term keeping. Salt serves the function of removing the moisture and acting as a preservative. You should use curing salt, a coarse noniodized salt, but any noniodized table salt will also do. Some vegetables may be salted also. A British woman described to me the family method used for preserving green beans when she was a child.

Take fresh-picked green beans from your garden. Wash them and allow them to drain until dry. Into a container, spread a layer of salt. Over the salt, place a layer of the green beans, then another layer of salt, alternating until the beans are gone, then covering all with a layer of salt. Before cooking, the beans may be soaked in one water to remove the excess salt.

To salt fish

1. Clean and wash fresh fish thoroughly. Scrape off scales and slime. Take off heads, fins, and tail. Take out guts; wash off blood. One teaspoon vinegar in a pan of clean water will help remove the slime.

2. Cut the fish into thin strips as for drying.

3. Scatter a layer of salt (about 35 pounds per 100 pounds fish, preferably coarse noniodized) over the bottom of the container. The container should be clean and of wood, plastic, or metal painted with fiberglass paint.

4. Place a layer of fish, flesh side up. Keep the layers as even and compact as possible.

5. Completely cover each layer of fish with salt.

6. Repeat steps **4** and **5** until the container is almost full.

7. The last layer should have the skin side up.

8. Top with a layer of salt.

9. Put a weight on the fish to be sure they stay under the brine which forms. Cover tightly.

10. At least ten to fourteen days are required to preserve the fish; longer in cool climates or if container is in a cool place.

11. You may repack the fish in a more convenient container by layering salt and fish, using only 10 pounds of salt to 100 pounds of fish for this repack.

12. Before using fish, soak overnight in clean water to remove salt.

Morton Salt Company offers a booklet called *A Complete Guide to Home Meat Curing.* (See *Suggested Reading.*)

SMOKING

Smoke thinly sliced meat rubbed with smoke salt over a fire built from green hardwood. Or convert an old refrigerator into a smoke-house by building a firebox where the motor was, with a vent to conduct the smoke to the shelving area. Filleted fish put on the shelves will be ready in 30 minutes.

JERKY

Follow instructions for drying meat in the preceding section. Rub thinly sliced meat with smoke salt, seasoned salt, and Liquid Smoke if desired, and dry in the oven at low heat until brittle.

PEMMICAN

Pemmican was made by the native American Indians, using jerky made by hanging meat slices on a pole or line to dry. Roast a dozen sticks of the resulting jerky until crisp. Put through a meat grinder, then add an equal amount of fine white suet from around calf kidneys (buffalo, if available). Mix in chokecherry pulp (sour cherry pulp is okay) and a little honey, if desired. Form into balls the size of chicken eggs. Place the balls in a can and cover with a little melted suet. Pemmican is extremely nourishing and will last indefinitely.

CELLARS, BASEMENTS, AND PITS

Many fruits and vegetables can be stored whole in a cool basement room or cellar, or by following the proper procedure, as shown on the chart on page 167. Winter squashes and pumpkins should first harden at 70° for a couple of weeks. Root vegetables should be kept in sand. Green tomatoes will ripen if individually wrapped in newspaper, boxed, and kept in a cool, dark place. Sort frequently and use the ripe ones for the table. I've kept fresh tomatoes until Christmas this way.

Your cold room should be 35° to 45°, dry with a little humidity, and must have ventilation.

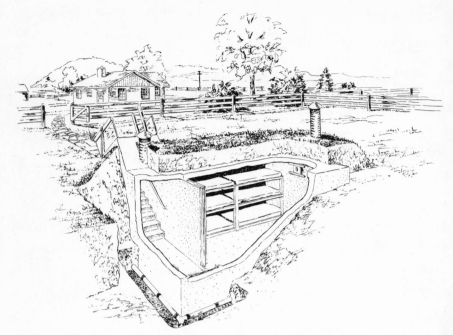

Underground cellar that can also serve as a storm and fallout shelter.

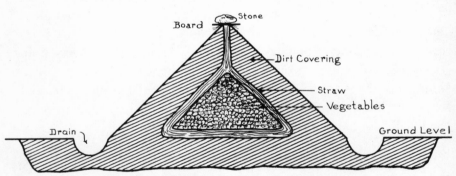

Cone-shaped pit showing details of construction.

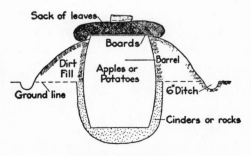

Barrel for storing.

Freezing Points, Recommended Storage Conditions, and Storage Length of Vegetables and Fruits

Food	Freezing Point (in °F.)	Place to Store	Storage Temperature (in °F.)	Conditions Humidity	Length of Storage Period
Vegetables					
Beans, dry	—	Any cool, dry place	32 to 40	Dry	As long as desired
Cabbage, late	30.4	Pit, trench, or outdoor cellar	As near 32 as possible	Moderately moist	Through late fall and winter
Cauliflower	30.3	Storage cellar	"	"	6 to 8 weeks
Celery, late	31.6	Pit or trench; roots in soil in storage cellar	"	"	Through late fall and winter
Endive	31.9	Roots in soil in storage cellar	"	"	2 to 3 months
Onions	30.6	Any cool, dry place	"	Dry	Through fall and winter
Parsnips	30.4	Where they grew, or in storage cellar	"	Moist	"
Peas, dry		Any cool, dry place	32-40	Dry	As long as desired
Potatoes	30.9	Pit or in storage cellar	35-40	"	Through fall and winter
Pumpkins	30.5	Home cellar or basement	55	Moderately dry	"
Root crops (miscellaneous)		Pit or in storage cellar	As near 32 as possible	Moist	"
Squashes	30.5	Home cellar or basement	55	Moderately dry	"
Sweet Potatoes	29.7	Home cellar or basement	55-60	Moderately dry	"
Tomatoes (mature green)	31.0	"	55-70	"	4 to 6 weeks
Fruits					
Apples	29.0	Fruit storage cellar	As near 32 as possible	Moderately moist	Through fall and winter
Grapefruit	29.8	"	"	"	4 to 6 weeks
Grapes	28.1	"	"	"	1 to 2 months
Oranges	30.5	"	"	"	4 to 6 weeks
Pears	29.2	"	"	"	Through fall and winter

SOURCE: "Storing Vegetables and Fruits," Home and Gardening Bulletin, No. 119, *U.S. Department of Agriculture.*

GARDENING

Your Garden

For the best nitty gritty foods, grow a garden. Your food will be more nutritious, because it's fresh and you will have improved your soil organically. You'll be healthier, not only from the good food you eat, but also from having tended the garden, thus exercising pleasantly outdoors.

You'll also save a lot of money and experience some incredible taste treats. There is no comparison between tasteless, woody tomatoes from the grocery and the sweet, juicy tomatoes you've picked and eaten in the garden on a sunny fall morning. Did you know that store-bought watermelons are watery and tasteless because their growth to enormous size is often speeded by injecting and forcing water consumption in numerous ways? They have no more sugar, however, than the sweet, smaller size from your garden, growing day by day in soil enriched by compost and carefully tended by you.

Gardening makes canning easier, too. Each day, harvest what is ripe; have it canned or frozen by noon. Of course, a good portion will be sidetracked to the table, and that's great. Kids (of all ages) love to go straight to the garden and select a healthful snack. I think my own children have not been so attached to empty foods because they've usually had access to a garden for munchies. When school is out in the summer and they're enjoying the outdoors, they'll often go to the garden for a raw treat.

A twenty-foot-square plot can grow quite a bit of food; a half an acre can supply a family of six for a year. A larger garden allows plenty for others—to give away, trade, or sell.

For your garden you'll need:

- Soil, spaded well for at least the first year. After that, spade at your discretion. Ruth Stout's no-work method claims spading only brings forth weed seeds and buries mulch needed more at the top of the soil.
- Sunlight at least most of the day.
- A sufficient water supply and a good irrigation system.
- Grass, hay, or straw for thick mulch between the rows to conserve moisture and keep down weeds. Let the thickness of the mulch grow as the plants grow. A thick mulch will allow you to water weekly instead of daily, and sometimes less frequently, depending on your soil and climate.
- A few tools. Start with shovel, hoe, and rake.
- Compost from your compost heap to enrich the soil.
- Friendly insects: ladybugs and praying mantises to control unfriendly creatures; earthworms for aerating the soil; bees for pollination. (Some crops have been known to produce ten times the harvest, once bees for pollination abounded.)
- Friendly plants: marigolds around the border to get rid of nematodes; garlic planted to discourage bugs.
- Dishes of beer and jars of syrup to catch insect pests.
- A cat to control chipmunks if they're a nuisance.
- A dog to chase away raccoons and rabbits, unless you grow enough extra to feed them.

- Banty chickens to gobble up insects. Banties won't harm the vegetables, whereas full-size chickens will scratch up the vegetables.
- A subscription to *Organic Gardening* Magazine.

Order seeds in February or March, selecting varieties from the large catalogs of W. Atlee Burpee Company, Gurney's Seeds, or any other nursery. It's best if you select a company in a location similar to yours, as the seeds will be better suited to your conditions. Do not save hybrid seeds from year to year—the plants will lose vitality. However, regular seeds from your choice plants can be saved. Collect them at the plant's top maturity. Then you'll gradually develop a strain of seeds best suited to your locale.

Plant the seeds that require a long growing season indoors during February and March, especially tomatoes and green peppers. Better still, start tender plants outdoors in hotbeds. One simple way to construct a hotbed is to form a square, using several thicknesses of straw bales. Put an old window across the top, raising it on warm days and lowering it at night and on chilly days.

Plant the other seeds outdoors after the date of the average last spring frost. Plant a little earlier if protected with mulching and plastic sheets.

After the soil is tilled and the seeds are planted and have germinated, there's not much to do, except keep mulching and composting and watching those plants grow. Just water occasionally, mulch, and harvest. The amount of work required will decrease as the amount of mulch and the strength of the plants increase. Healthy organic plants withstand bugs and diseases better than sickly plants.

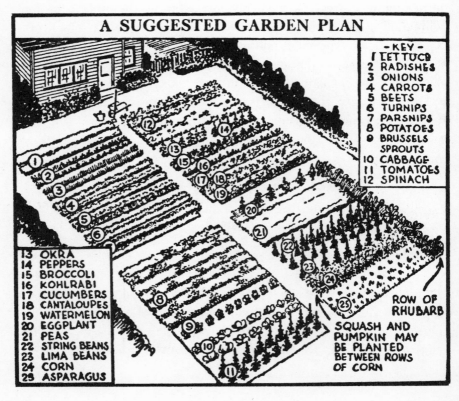

A SUGGESTED GARDEN PLAN

- KEY -
1 LETTUCE
2 RADISHES
3 ONIONS
4 CARROTS
5 BEETS
6 TURNIPS
7 PARSNIPS
8 POTATOES
9 BRUSSELS SPROUTS
10 CABBAGE
11 TOMATOES
12 SPINACH

13 OKRA
14 PEPPERS
15 BROCCOLI
16 KOHLRABI
17 CUCUMBERS
18 CANTALOUPES
19 WATERMELON
20 EGGPLANT
21 PEAS
22 STRING BEANS
23 LIMA BEANS
24 CORN
25 ASPARAGUS

ROW OF RHUBARB

SQUASH AND PUMPKIN MAY BE PLANTED BETWEEN ROWS OF CORN

Gurney's Planting Chart For Vegetables

Vegetables	Amt. Seed to 50 ft. row	Depth (in.)	Rows apart (in.)	Inches apart in row after thinning	When to plant	Probable yield from 50 ft. row
Asparagus	2 pkts.	1 in.	40 in.	15	Mar.-Apr.	17 lbs.
Bush Beans	½ lb.	2 in.	20 in.	4	Apr.-May	¾ bu.
Pole Beans	½ lb.	2 in.	48 in.	48	Apr.-May	1 bu.
Table Beets	2 pkts.	1 in.	12 in.	4	Mar.-Apr.	1 bu.
Mangel Beets	1 oz.	1 in.	12 in.	4	Mar.-Apr.	75 lbs.
Broccoli	⅛ oz.	½ in.	36 in.	18	Apr.-May	50 lbs.
Brussels Sprouts	⅛ oz.	½ in.	36 in.	18	Apr.-May	15 qts.
Cabbage-early	½ oz.	½ in.	36 in.	16	Mar.-Apr.	75 lbs.
Cabbage-late	½ oz.	1 in.	36 in.	16	Apr.-May	100 lbs.
Carrots	2 pkts.	½ in.	12 in.	½	Mar.-Apr.	1 bu.
Cauliflower	2 pkts.	½ in.	36 in.	18	Mar.-Apr.	30 heads
Cucumbers	2 pkts.	1 in.	6 ft.	4 ft.	Apr.-May	50 lbs.
Eggplants	2 pkts.	¼ in.	36 in.	24	Apr.-May	60 fruits
Endive	2 pkts.	½ in.	12 in.	Don't thin	Apr.-May	25 lbs.
Garlic Cloves	1 lb.	1 in.	18 in.	3	Mar.-Apr.	1 bu.
Kale	1 pkt.	½ in.	18 in.	6	Mar.-Apr.	2 bu.
Kohlrabi	2 pkts.	½ in.	18 in.	3	Mar.-Apr.	40 lbs.
Lettuce	2 pkts.	½ in.	12 in.	4	Mar.-Apr.	35 lbs.
Muskmelons	2 pkts.	1 in.	5 ft.	3 ft.	May	35 fruits
Mustard	2 pkts.	¼ in.	24 in.	12	Aug.	1 bu.
Onion (seed)	2 pkts.	1 in.	12 in.	4	Mar.-Apr.	1 bu.
Onion (sets)	1 qt.	2 in.	12 in.	2	Mar.-Apr.	1 bu.
Parsnips	1 pkt.	¼ in.	18 in.	3	Apr.-May	1 bu.
Peas	½ lb.	2 in.	24 in.	4	Apr.-May	1 bu.
Peppers	1 pkt.	¼ in.	3 ft.	3 ft.	Apr.-May	150 fruits
Potato white	50 sets	4 in.	30 in.	12	Mar.-Apr.	2 bu.
Popcorn	1 pkt.	1 in.	36 in.	12	Apr.-May	50 lbs.
Pumpkins	2 pkts.	1 in.	8 ft.	8 ft.	May	45 fruits
Radishes	2 pkts.	½ in.	12 in.	2	Mar.-Apr.	50 lbs.
Rhubarb	25 roots	3 in.	36 in.	24	Apr.-May	150 stalks
Rutabaga	2 pkts.	½ in.	36 in.	3	Apr.-May	50 lbs.
Salsify	½ oz.	¾ in.	12 in.	2	Mar.-Apr.	1 bu.
Spinach	2 pkts.	¾ in.	12 in.	4	Apr.-May	4 lbs.
Squash	2 pkts.	1 in.	8 ft.	8 ft.	May	30 fruits
Sweet Corn	1 pkt.	2 in.	36 in.	12	May	48 ears
Swiss Chard	1 pkt.	1 in.	36 in.	18	Apr.	35 lbs.
Tomato Hybrids	2 pkts.	½ in.	48 in.	48	Apr.-May	3 bu.
Turnips	2 pkts.	1 in.	12 in.	4	Apr.-May	1 bu.
Watermelons	2 pkts.	1 in.	8 ft.	8 ft.	May	15 fruits

Protect from early frosts in the fall by using mulch and plastic tarps on nights when frost threatens. Be sure to remove any covering when the temperature rises. The garden's growing time and production can often be increased by a month or more with careful tending. When nights get too cold for the individual plants to survive with only a plastic cover, uproot tomato plants, squashes, and melons and pile them in high piles, then cover the piles with tarps. This method will allow some of the fruit to continue to vine-ripen. Pumpkins, dry beans, and onions can be left in the ground until after the first light frost. Uproot dried bean vines and spread on a blanket. Beat with a broom until the beans fall off on the blanket. Shortly before the first frost is expected, step on onion tops and allow them to dry out. Harvest at frost time and braid the onions together, if desired, braiding the tops along with a piece of twine. Hang the string in a cool dry place. Carrots and turnips can be left in the ground all winter if mulched heavily, and providing your winters are not severe. Dig them up as needed. Parsnips should winter over underground. Cabbages, broccoli, and

Brussels sprouts survive light frosts quite well. Lettuce can be planted before the last frost in the spring and will hardily survive mild frosts.

Many old-timers claim other factors can help your garden, among them love for the plants and planting by the moon. I myself feel plants respond to caring and careful attention, just as animals do. Perhaps the key to a green thumb is a warm heart. However, there is a limit to what a warm heart alone can do, at least in ordinary experience.

I've tried planting by the moon and have had amazing results. I don't know why, but here's how I've tested the idea: I planted some tomato seeds at the absolutely maximal time (Sun in Pisces, Moon waxing in Cancer) and they germinated in two or three days, grew rapidly, and were some of the healthiest plants I ever saw. The same season, I planted some tomato seeds (same seeds, same soil) at the worst astrological time (Sun in Aries, Moon fourth quarter in Leo), and they germinated sparsely in ten days to two weeks. They were weak and poor plants, too. There was a definite difference—maybe I rooted for the first batch. Anyway, the way the rule works, if you'd like to try it, is: water signs (Pisces, Cancer, Scorpio) are the most fertile; earth signs next (Capricorn, Taurus, Virgo); air signs next (Aquarius, Gemini, Libra); and fire signs last (Aries, Leo, Sagittarius). First and second quarters while the moon is growing are good for planting; third quarter is considered good for root crops; and fourth quarter is suitable only for weeding and other destruction. There are several variations, but this is the basic scheme. I believe we need all the help we can get. As Hamlet said, "There are more things in heaven and earth, Horatio, than are dreamt of in your philosophy."

Dung Barrow

The Compost Heap

Save every scrap of organic garbage for your compost heap—from vegetable trimmings to hair clippings. Your best sources are straw and manure from animal stalls, trimmings from fruits and vegetables, neighbors' leaves and grass clippings. Add a little bone and blood meal. Accumulate compost in piles of a cubic yard, keep it moist, and turn it occasionally. Keep the compost heap covered with a sheet of plastic to hold in the heat and moisture and to keep out insects. The internal temperature will go way up and destroy insect larvae; the pile will steam on snowy days. We've sunned ourselves on some icy-cold winter afternoons sitting on the huge black-plastic-covered compost heap, so warm you could feel the heat through the seat of your pants.

In a month, sometimes more, you'll have rich, black humus; quicker if you have some way to shred composting material, if you have friendly earthworms helping the digestion, and if you have a sufficient variety and quantity of rich organic matter. That finished humus will not only look good, but will smell great, and will do wonders for your plants. You can almost see them perk up when they know it's coming!

Minigardens

So you've just wistfully read the gardening section, but are wondering how you can use the information, there in your city apartment. However, if you have a doorstep, a balcony, or a windowsill, you have enough space for a minigarden. If a patio or a roof is available, all the better.

For minigardening, you'll need some containers, some soil, some fertilizer (preferably compost), and some seeds. The container you choose must be large enough to hold the full-grown plant. Try clay pots, an old pail, a bushel basket, a plastic bucket or pot, or a wooden box. Six-inch pots are fine for chives. Radishes, onions, and miniature tomatoes do well in 10-inch pots. Five-gallon plastic

Watering Pot.

trash cans are suitable for the average patio and provide space for larger vegetable plants. Half-bushel or bushel baskets also work well for larger plants. Build your own containers, if you wish.

Solid plastic containers must have four or more quarter-inch holes drilled for drainage. These holes should be placed in the side, near the bottom, and spaced evenly. Place a half inch of coarse gravel in the bottom of each container. Paint wood containers inside and out with a safe wood preservative and they will last a long time.

Buy a potting soil, or mix your own. To 1 bushel each of vermiculite and shredded peat moss, add 1-1/4 cups of ground limestone (preferably dolomitic) and several cups of compost, or 1/2 cup of 20% superphosphate and 1 cup of 5-10-5 fertilizer. Mix the material thoroughly, adding a little water to reduce the dust if necessary.

Choose seeds that are stamped with the date of the current year. Choose miniature varieties. Vegetable fruit plants, such as cucumbers, peppers, and tomatoes, need the most sunlight. Root vegetables get by with a little less. Leafy vegetables, such as lettuce, cabbage, and greens, can get along with more shade than root vegetables.

Begin plants indoors on windowsills that have plenty of sunlight, then transplant them into larger containers after the weather warms. Use peat pots or milk cartons slit sideways for starting seedlings. "Harden" or toughen the plants for two weeks before moving them outdoors. Do this by watering little and lowering the temperature to prepare them for the temperature extremes and wind of outdoors. When transplanting your seedlings, be careful not to disturb the roots.

Apply fresh compost or other organic fertilizer every three weeks. Mix the fertilizer into the top of the soil and water thoroughly. Give vegetables water equal to about an inch of rain every week during the growing season. Water when the soil becomes dry to a depth of 1/8 inch. Watering well and less frequently will cause your plants to develop a good root structure. Overwatering will kill your plants. Pull any weeds that come up, and loosen the topsoil in your containers with a fork from time to time, being careful not to disturb the plant.

Larger scale minigardens can be grown on rooftops or in vertical planter walls. Obtaining soil and insuring proper drainage are the primary problems for rooftop gardeners. Root vegetables will require deeper soil than will leafy vegetables. If the space is available, large boxes can be built to hold the soil for growing a variety of vegetables. An experimental program of the Brooklyn Botanic Garden indicates a substantial amount of vegetables can be grown on eighty square feet of rooftop space.

To grow vegetables in vertical planter walls, begin by constructing a sturdy yard-square (or more) frame, 6 to 8 inches deep. Surround this with 2-inch wire mesh. One side only can be left open, or both sides can be left open if desired. Firmly pack your planter wall with sphagnum moss. Then insert seedlings in holes between the wire mesh. Make the holes at a slightly downward angle. Since you're planting in the yard-square vertical space, the plants will not spread as they will in a horizontal bed, so many plants will fit into the space.

The wall must remain evenly moist throughout, but not wet. A soaker hose placed across the top will water evenly. Stop watering when water comes out the bottom of the container. Fertilize every two weeks with water that has been soaking with compost or manure (manure tea), or use a complete, preferably organic, fertilizer in the watering solution.

A vertical planter wall planted with flowers is exquisite. Strawberries, kitchen herbs, and garden vegetables such as lettuce and spinach grow well in a planter wall. A vertical garden of this type makes a nice outdoor screen from close neighbors.

For further information on minigardening, consult the Brooklyn Botanic Garden's handbook called *Gardening in Containers*. (See *Suggested Reading.*)

KEEPING SMALL LIVESTOCK

Chickens

Chickens are remarkably easy to raise—if you keep a small flock.

For your family of five, we have two to three dozen hens and a couple of roosters. Undoubtedly a dozen would suffice, as we usually have eggs for other people, too. Although three dozen chickens may sound like a lot of birds, they really take very little space and effort.

Our chickens run free. They are able to be free because our dogs protect them from marauding animals. Also, Big Red, the top rooster, has been known to chase dogs seventy-five feet down the road. Without this protection they would have to stay in a pen. They would also have to have their wings clipped so they couldn't fly over the fence.

Because they are free to seek whatever food they desire, they are fat and very healthy. Some of the hens are three or four years old, yet they still lay eggs regularly, although not as often as do the younger hens. We have approximately thirty hens, and we have had as many as 28 eggs in one day. However, the average hen lays 200 to 240 eggs per year.

The chickens have grown so tame that when we open our front door in the morning about a dozen come running to greet us. Most of them have names. Natasha and Little Red Hen like to be held. Clara Cluck and Victoria were sisterly-sweet elderly

grannies in bronze shawls who have since gone to the great chickenhouse in the sky.

I am quite sure that little of our chicken-raising philosophy would be considered orthodox by agricultural experts. Yet we are incredibly successful with these few chickens, with only makeshift facilities for them, but with careful attention to other aspects of their care.

Our three dozen chickens share a dry, though drafty, indoor area which is about 4 x 10 feet. This includes roosting bars to hold them all two to three feet off the ground. On the few days that are too cold and wet they stay inside; they hop in with the goats and gossip on a shelf above the goats' heads. Ideally, the area beneath the roosts should be screened from their access because that's where the droppings fall.

A much larger chicken house should be provided if the birds are to be confined inside, allowing three square feet or more each. If they can't scratch outside, grit should be provided, also. I simply do not recommend confining chickens in a coop without a run.

Our chickens are very hardy, and we find they only stay inside if the temperature is below zero, or if a blinding snowstorm or pouring rain is in progress. Most of our winter days are cold, but the sun shines. If you live in an area that is continually very cold and wet, you'll need a larger coop.

When the temperature dropped to 35° below for three nights, we took the edge off the cold in our little barn with a camping catalytic heater, hung securely to prevent fire hazard and to keep from burning the animals. Despite our drafty barn and the miserable weather, among all those chickens only one comb and one toe were very slightly frostbitten during that cold spell. One elderly hen who wasn't faring well was brought inside the house. That was Natasha, who has since been almost a nuisance with her loyalty and affection. (But we like it!)

Chickens are natural foragers. Almost any scraps the goats don't want, the chickens will eat. Furthermore, they spend a lot of time scratching on the compost pile looking for food. They help keep the compost aerated and turned, and they help keep the bug population down by eating young insects as they hatch. I think hens like the compost heap for the lovely food delicacies they find there, and also because it's the warmest spot on a cold day.

The chickens are good companions for the goats. They get along well. Sometimes, especially when the weather is cold, a couple of chickens will sit in the sun on a goat's back. They have also been known to ride the goats. They carefully gather up the grain and scraps the goats waste. But we do keep them penned separately at night, because chickens are almost blind in the dark and the goats are careless about where they lie down.

The feed usually fed chickens is called "lay mash" or "scratch." Either of these is good feed if carefully fed in regular chicken feeders. But sometimes we like to scatter coarse feed for the chickens, and for this purpose mash and scratch are too fine and a lot would be wasted. Also, I find the scratch too low in protein.

So usually our chickens are fed the goats' dairy ration or a higher protein horse feed of mixed grains. They seem to flourish on it, although I must mention that the chicken feeds are formulated especially for top chicken production. New chicks also must have growing mash continuously.

All our chickens have been organically fed and raised. They have never been confined, nor have they been forced to lay with extra lighting or hormones or amphetamines. Eventually I hope to mix their feed myself and to get away from purchased feed, which does have nonorganic material in it. Your local Department of Agriculture farm agent will give you advice free of charge on the proper mix for your situation.

Our chickens lay eggs winter and summer. Like all chickens, their top productivity is in the spring. But unlike most chickens, the only days last winter they did not lay were a few when the weather was way below zero. Their laying did diminish, but there were always plenty of eggs for the family. Hens usually quit laying for weeks in the winter.

Hens like to find a quiet and preferably dark spot to lay their eggs. A box with a six-inch hole cut out of the side makes a good nest box. There should be one box for every four hens. Gather the eggs twice a day to insure freshness. Wipe them clean and refrigerate, pointed end down. Do not scrub them, as you'll take away the protective coating that preserves their quality until used.

Before being cultivated as domestic animals, hens probably laid only a dozen eggs a year, in the spring. As soon as a dozen were accumulated, the hen would sit on the eggs until her chicks hatched. Then she didn't lay until the next year. Perhaps our laying hens today are still making a wholehearted attempt to gather together a dozen eggs for hatching. Each day the faithful hen begins to lay again as she finds her nest empty.

When we add a few new chickens to our flock each summer to assure a constant supply of young layers, we end up with extra roosters. These we butcher and eat. But our primary reason for keeping chickens is for the eggs. We never eat our hens—it seems foolish to have a hen for a meal, when with nurturing she would give many meals during her laying span.

It does make economic sense to eat the hens after their laying has diminished, but by that time ours have become part of the family. Besides, after all the faithful service, we feel we should take care of them in their old age. I suppose if we were hungry enough our minds would change. But for the time being, there's a clear line drawn between the laying hens and the extra roosters intended for meat. Someday, when we have more space, we'll raise more roosters for fryers.

The best way to add to the flock is by allowing a sitting hen to hatch chicks. A small percentage of hens, usually the older ones, will make their own decision to brood. Then, if you allow them to remain on a nest, in twenty-one days baby chicks will hatch. If a hen hatches only a few babies, she will probably allow you to sneak in a few extra chicks from the hatchery.

A broody hen will save you lots of work. She will remain on the nest night and day, except for feeding, and will do her best to protect the nest and hatch the chicks. She is not dependent on technology, like an electric incubator.

After the baby chicks are hatched, she nurses the chicks along until they are able to take care of themselves. She protects them from the rest of the flock. She covers them with her wings and huddles over them to keep the chicks warm and dry if the weather is bad.

However, one hen can't hatch and care for as many baby chicks as an incubator and brooder, so the decision hinges on how many new additions you want. The fertile eggs from your own chickens can be hatched and cared for by incubator and brooder, and, of course, you.

CHICK BROODING

Get ready for the arrival of your chicks well in advance by thoroughly cleaning the poultry house and all equipment. Have feeders and waterers filled and brooder temperature adjusted before the chicks arrive. The first week, the brooder temperature should be 90 to 95° F. two inches above the litter. Reduce the temperature 5° per week until 70° is reached. Keep the brooder regulated to a temperature at which the chicks seem comfortable.

Allow each chick a minimum of 7 square inches under the brooder. Allow 1/2 square foot of brooder room floor space per chick through six weeks, then a minimum of one square foot per bird through 12 weeks.

Be sure chicks are not crowded either at feeders or at waterers. Use long, thin feeders for best spacing. Absolutely avoid overcrowding in hot weather.

In cold weather, use a solid guard around the brooder hood to prevent chicks from straying and to prevent drafts. A wire guard is suitable in warm weather. The guard should be placed two or three feet from the edge of the hood. It should be removed after one week. Provide roosts at four weeks of age, allowing 4 inches of space per chick.

Provide at least a two-inch depth of litter at the beginning. Sawdust, shavings, and similar material may be used if free of harmful substances and fine dust.

Be sure that the lighting and heat for the chicks are distributed so they don't all cluster in one location.

Feed new chicks as soon as possible by spreading chick starter on papers or lids under the brooder. Keep grit available.

Prevent cannibalism by allowing plenty of space, food, and water. Admit only subdued light. Use an anti-pick salve if necessary.

Baby chicks and all supplies are available from Sears' and Ward's farm catalogs. However, it may be better to get chicks a few weeks old from a local reliable hatchery or feed store. Older chicks are stronger and not so susceptible to all the hassles that plague baby chicks. The older they are, the more expensive they are. And pullets (females) are more expensive than cockerels (males).

I have a good arrangement with a family that does organic farming on a small scale. They raise a few chicks for me along with theirs, as they have complete equipment and are set up to handle the problems. I bring the chicks home when they've feathered out, about a month old.

Dame Partlet's Farm

When buying chicks or chickens, buy a breed that best suits your needs. Some, like White Rocks, are meant for meat and grow to greater poundage. Some, like Leghorn, are bred for egg production and have less meat. I have excellent egg production from a breed called Calhorn. They produced their first eggs at five months and have been going strong ever since, more reliable than the postman. One rooster is all you need for every fifteen or twenty hens.

Be sure to keep fresh water available for your chickens at all times. In winter, warm water will help egg production. Also, feed them crushed oyster shell (available at your local feed store) from time to time to provide calcium for hard-shelled eggs. Or keep a little accessible at all times in a clean place.

Beware of a big chicken flock—unless you really want to get into the chicken business. We find forty chickens to be about maximum. After that, you lose touch with them as individuals. They become simply the poultry flock—more work and less pleasure, with problems increasing geometrically, or so it seems to me.

The one nuisance our chickens have had is common among chickens. These are chicken mites, tiny bugs that crawl beneath the feathers. They do need to be controlled, as they will spread from chicken to chicken, are irritating, and cause the general health and laying to be somewhat diminished. So far I have been unable to find an organic method of getting rid of chicken mites. So I have used chicken mite powder when necessary. However, they will return, and a few are to be expected in any case, so don't panic. The mite problem and other health problems can be partially avoided or mitigated by keeping chickens away from their droppings by screening under and around the bottom of the roosts.

Another common chicken problem is pecking each other. If the problem gets serious, they will peck eyes and even kill each other. This can be partially resolved by giving them a block of Weysol to peck on. But my chickens never peck each other, except gently, when they're grooming for mites. I suspect the pecking problem may be a result of crowding, boredom, and diet without variety.

Chicken diseases can be pretty serious. If any of your chickens become sick, consult a veterinary book or a veterinarian. Some chicken diseases can quickly wipe out entire flocks. Diseases vary considerably in symptoms and treatment.

However, I find that by letting the chickens live a normal, free life with good food, sunshine, fresh air, and exercise, they remain amazingly healthy. Ours have been practically problem-free. I am also very careful about adding any new outside chickens to the flock, as that is the way some diseases come in. I think it is likely that a small, stable flock is more apt to be healthy.

Let your chickens live as happily and naturally as you can. They'll love you for it, and give many eggs as the reward. We find chickens sensitive to the attention and love we give them. We've even been known to sing them an egg-laying song in scarce-egg times, and they have responded with lots of yummy, fresh eggs. What's an egg-laying song? Just sit with them, watch them, and talk with them. Then sing them an egg-inspiring song. I sing mine, "Somewhere my hens...are laying many eggs" and so on. The chorus, of course, goes "Braawwk, braawwk, brawk, brawk." Really!

Goats

A milking goat has got to be one of the most efficient and ingenious creatures that man has to supply food.

A good milking goat will give three to four quarts of milk each day, ten months of the year. She will be your friend and pet. She will follow you on a walk, nuzzling you as you go down the road. She will carry saddlebags for you if you backpack. She will provide manure and old straw bedding to make your compost heap a dynamic, rich one. She will stay healthy and productive on land that would nearly starve a lizard. She will browse contentedly on steep, rocky slopes or thick brush. She will pay for most of her grain with the kids she gives annually.

She will eat your lilacs. She will baa to be fed on time the day you decide to sleep late. She would rather live in the house with the humans than in the barnyard with the livestock.

Goats have a strange appearance. They look like a sculptural armature around which has been arranged a sack of skin. The skin has been filled at random with odd bulges and undulations.

Goats behave oddly, but their strange reputation is somewhat different than the real facts. "They eat tin cans." "They smell." "They're mean." "Their milk tastes bad." "They're stupid." My comments about these rumors follow, one by one.

They do not eat tin cans. But they do eat some pretty strange things. Mine have occasionally been known to eat a piece of plastic or someone else's cigarette butt. Well, they're good sanitation engineers. Their favorite food is tree leaves, and they'll occasionally eat the bark, especially to self-treat indigestion. They love good hay and alfalfa and fresh vegetables. They're picky eaters and won't eat anything they consider dirty.

They rarely smell. A nanny goat will have an unpleasant odor only if her yard and barn are kept in horrendous condition. Most nannies have a nice, warm, hay-barn-milk scent.

Billy goats can be another story, especially in the fall when they are in "rut," their mating season. During that time glands between their horns secrete a musky goop, and the bucks will behave in a pretty gross manner.

Goats are generally very gentle. When ours are out to browse we have to watch them closely; sometimes they follow strangers up the road. They follow us around like puppies. On nice days they lay with the dogs beside the back door, contentedly chewing their cuds. They'd like to come indoors and will try. I've heard they can be paper-trained, but I keep having visions of a goat leaping onto my table like the family cat! Our nannies never butt us. But they do a lovely dance with each other in which they balance on their hind legs and bump heads. After they've had their first kids and are feeling protective, the nannies will be quite firm with most dogs, chasing ill-mannered dogs out of the yard.

The billies are more aggressive than the nannies and might actually butt you in the seat of the pants. But they generally mean no harm. Their behavior when adult is directly related to their interaction with you when they were kids. In a couple of years, your billy kid will weigh two or three hundred pounds. Treat him accordingly: don't encourage more friskiness than you can handle when he becomes full grown. After all, he can't be expected to know that the reason you don't play rough with him any longer is because he's a physical threat. Plan to keep him confined or on the north forty when he's in rut and especially obnoxious.

Our goats' milk tastes as good or better than fresh cows' milk. Some commercial goats' milk I've had tastes ghastly, so don't judge by what you buy. Off-taste milk is usually caused by bad feed, a smelly barn, an odiferous buck too close to the nannies, manure-tainted hooves that need trimming, improper care of the milk, or old milk. There is a difference in goats, too.

The milk you get from your goats will be fresh and fine, poured from a misty, pottery pitcher on a hot summer's day. See that your goats eat sweet feed, clean the barn regularly, keep hooves trimmed, wash the buck's head, and separate him from the nannies. Immediately after milking, refrigerate your strained milk in a carefully washed or sterilized container with a tight lid. Milk is quick to pick up odd tastes from bad odors.

I have not written a section on cows because this book is about everything that can easily be done on one acre or less.

However, I personally prefer goats to cows, having had experience with both. To me, some of the advantages of goats over cows are:

● Low initial investment. The cost of mixed-breed begins at about $15 and milking nannies about $50, depending on quality and age; purebreds cost much more. But the production of a good mixed breed could be equal to or even superior to that of a purebred. Cows are much more expensive.

● Little equipment and space are needed. A larger barn, larger pen, and more grazing space are needed for cows.

● Easy clean-up of handy pelletized manure, great for the compost heap. (You'll know what I mean if you've ever cleaned a cow barn!)

● Easy milking and no need to herd them in. Just "baa," and they'll come running and jump right up on the milking bench.

● Low feed cost and higher milk production for feed dollar. We spend under ten dollars a month for grain for three. However, feed costs vary. Feeding goats alfalfa cuts down or eliminates their need for grain.

● Goats' milk is better for human digestion than cows' milk. It's also recommended for many people with allergies to cows' milk.

● Goats are easier to handle. All our children can feed and milk them—a ten year old can handle milking and goat care. A balky cow, or especially a bull, is very difficult for one person to handle. Did you ever have a cow step on your foot?

● Goats are more resistant to disease. They are not susceptible to tuberculosis or other diseases cattle commonly get. Most goat diseases are not transmittable to humans, unlike cow diseases. This is an important consideration, especially if you drink raw milk. (It's still a good idea to get your milk tested twice a year. Ask your County Agent to suggest someone.)

● Better adaptability to environment. Our goats graze on land that would starve a cow and break her legs. The goats scamper over the rocks and feed with ease.

● Ever try to take a cow in your family car to be bred? Ha! A goat will hop right in. Or think of leading a half-ton-plus bull as compared to a 200-pound billy. Quite a difference!

● A block and tackle are standard equipment in difficult calf deliveries. Imagine that. Believe me, you'll never have to use a block and tackle to deliver a goat, and you'll rarely have a goat with any difficulty in delivering.

● Does your family have use for the two or three gallons of milk given daily by the average cow? The three quarts to one gallon given daily by one goat is better geared to family consumption.

• Some people feel cows are more placid, with better dispositions. Well, most goats I've known are personable and gentle. But they are strong individuals and not necessarily placid. You can always name your goat "Bossy," if it will satisfy your longing.

• If all fails, it's much easier to dispose of the body of a dead goat!

The disadvantages of goat-keeping include:

• Goats are hard to confine. They'll try their best to find a way out if they're not content.

• You can't ride them. I've ridden a cow or two in my past. (A billy goat can be taught to pull a cart or small plow.)

• They refuse to be treated like livestock. If you don't genuinely like them, keeping goats won't work.

Most of the other hassles will be about the same as you'd have with cows:

• They'll eat your flowers and bushes if they get a chance.

• They need to be cared for daily; you'll have to get an animal sitter if you are traveling. During milking season you'll have to milk twice daily whether you want to or not if you expect the milk production to remain stable. Some days you'll feel, as the Nearings and Thoreau both mention, that life could be simpler without animals. However, we have been fortunate in always having a neighbor or two who like animals and are happy to care for them in exchange for the milk.

What do goats need?

1. A shelter from bad weather and a pen. The barn should provide a shelter from wet weather and be at minimum a windbreak. Goats can stand lots of cold and will grow thick fur in response to cold weather, but they should not get wet. Young kids will quickly develop pneumonia if they are not kept dry. Our billy, who currently has poor shelter, gets absolutely shaggy in winter.

Our goats sleep in a rough barn that's small in size. In the barn is a big wooden box on its side. The top of the box is fixed as a milking stanchion, with a smaller box used as a step to help the nannies hop on it. Our milk stand looks like this:

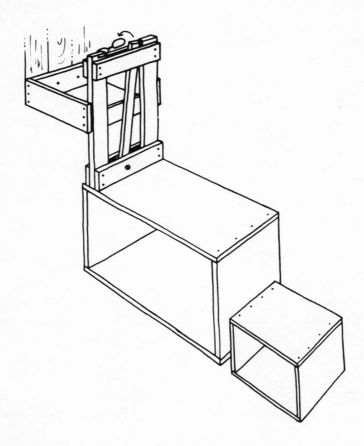

A raised stanchion, depending on its height, allows the milker to sit or stand in a comfortable position. A fellow once asked me what was the hardest part about keeping goats. I answered him, "Crawling underneath them morning and night in order to milk." And he believed me!

A stanchion should provide a raised area for the goat to stand on while being milked, a place for grain to be fed while milking, and some means of confinement or attachment. Below are two suggested ways to confine the animal while milking:

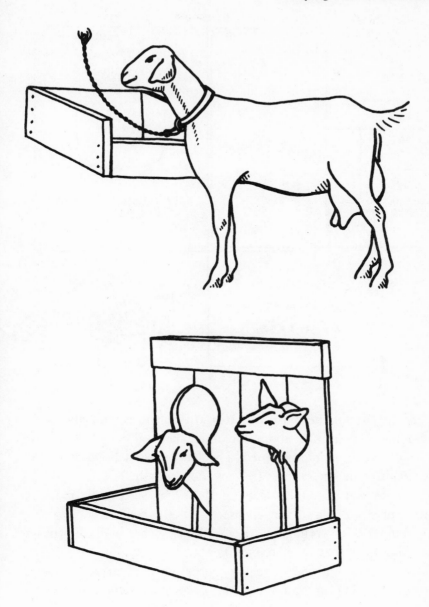

The open space under our stanchion, which is the open part of the large box, we use as a kid box. That is where the kids sleep until they are too big. This way we utilize all our small space.

An excellent barn I know looks like this:

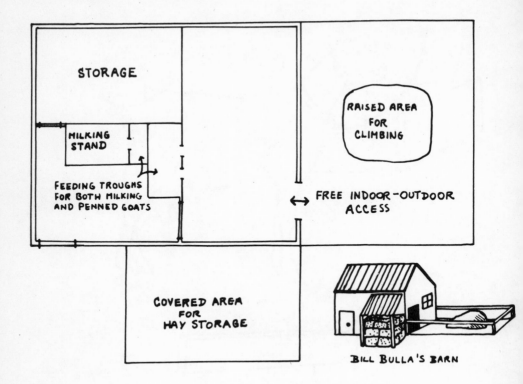

Fencing around the barn, the area where you confine the goats, should allow plenty of room for movement, although goats are not wildly active while confined. The fence should be very sturdy, and the best height is five feet or more. If she chooses, one of my nannies can gracefully leap our four-foot fence with room to spare. But she doesn't often choose to.

A standard low-voltage livestock electric fence will discourage a jumping goat that must remain confined—if nothing else works.

The nannies will not attack a fence with vigor; they spend their time trying to figure out the gate latch. But our billy is more overt. If he can't open the latch, he will just brutally bash the fence with his head until he breaks a hole. He once put his head through very heavy gauge wire. I've often felt a suitable fence for a big billy would be constructed of railroad ties.

For temporary or nomadic confinement to a specific area, goats may be tethered. However, they might eat almost any organic tether. So for the nannies I use a thin, long chain, about the weight of a dog leash. A chain works fine for a billy, too, but it must be much heavier. These can be attached to the goat's collar on the goat end and to a pivot or running wire on the other end, like this:

The goats' collars should be made of leather rather than chain, so that they are more comfortable. The collar gives something to hang onto while leading the goat.

2. Good food. I find more varied the feed, the healthier the goat. We feed ours hay, grain overripe vegetables and fruits, grass clippings, and tree leaves. They will, however, not be inclined to eat dirty food, and it's best if their food does'nt touch the ground. Nannies, especially, are very dainty eaters, except for the oddities they occasionally indulge in.

They prefer hay with little straw, and they do like alfalfa, which has more protein than grass. Feed only as much hay as they'll eat in a couple of hours. Once it's dirty, they won't touch it. Be sure to include plenty of hay and alfalfa in feeding during the winter. Grains alone do not allow a goat's metabolism to produce sufficient body heat. Build a manger for feeding hay that looks like this:

In the spring, gradually introduce green feed into the diet, so they don't bloat. If the goats are free to graze, they'll gradually become accustomed to the slowly greening vegetation. However, feed them before turning them out to graze. Then they'll avoid food that is not good for them, such as chokeberry leaves and branches. Most of these things won't hurt them if they've had something else to eat first. By the way, goats carefully leave an inch or so of grass as they graze, unlike sheep.

A horse ration works well for feeding goats. And remember, your milking nannies must be fed a dairy ration to replace minerals that go into milk production. Otherwise minerals will be drawn from their bones to make up the deficit. A high content of whole corn should not be fed, as it grinds down the teeth.

Feed a handful of calf ration to young kids. Milkers get one pound of grain for every two quarts of milk production.

Your billy need not get grain daily if he's on good pasture. But if his variety of feed is limited, he should be given a little grain daily. He cannot produce good offspring if he's in poor health.

Keep grain rations in a goatproof place. Covered garbage cans work well if the lids are secured with tie-downs. Goats are smart enough to try anything to get the grain they love so well, and greedy enough to eat until they bloat and die.

We pick up overripe vegetables and fruits from the produce man at the grocery. These are thrown away anyhow, and they mean better health and higher milk production to your goats. If you have chickens, they will forage for the leftovers. Just be sure not to feed strong-tasting vegetables like onions to milking goats, as they will affect the taste of the milk.

I gather bags of fresh (not spoiled) grass clippings, dry rakings, and fall leaves for my goats from city folks. Be sure the grass clippings and yard rakings come from nonsprayed lawns. If the grass or leaves are dry, they can be kept in bags for later feeding. If they are damp, they must be used right away, or spread to dry in the sun. Each fall I haul dozens of bags of leaves and stack them, to cut down on the cost of hay. Besides, leaves are a real delicacy to goats.

For grazing and browsing, your goats will flourish on most any kind of vegetation. A good meadow or dry scrubby land will suit them. They will even prune thorny raspberry plants in fall and spring, and happily eat poison ivy, which hurts neither them nor their milk. (In fact, some people claim they've been immunized temporarily against poison ivy by drinking milk from goats who've fed on it. But I don't think this idea has been tested, so I can't recommend it.) Most of our land is vertical and seemingly barren, except for pines and small wild plants. Yet our goats look lean when let out in the morning and come to be milked in the evening with their sides bulging out, content as can be.

A salt lick must be kept available at all times. (Sulphur salt will keep away ticks.) Water must also be kept available at all times, or milk production will drop. In winter, goats appreciate receiving warm water, or an electric device can be purchased to keep the water thawed. In summer, goats drink a tremendous quantity of water. If you can devise a way for water to trickle slowly into a bucket at all times, this works best.

3. Goats are extremely social creatures and require some sort of companionship, whether other goats, livestock, or humans. A solitary goat can be a miserable creature.

The old expression "Get your goat" has the following background. Nanny goats are often kept with racehorses, as they are soothing company. A nasty competitor would steal the goat on the day of the race, disconcerting the horse to such an extent that he would lose the race. Hence, "Get your goat."

4. Goats do require regular care. They cannot be cared for in a slipshod manner. If you are going to keep them, then you must be responsible to them.

They like to be milked at approximately the same time each day. Daylight savings time is a muddle to them—they continue on their own time and slowly adjust. They should be fed and given fresh water twice a day. Trim hooves down to the pale pink area monthly if your goats don't wear them down on rocks.

The pen and barn should be cleaned regularly. All waste removed from the pen should be put on the compost pile. Some authorities suggest a cement-floor barn; I feel they are cold and hard on the goats' feet, but they are easier to hose down. In any case, the barn floor should be kept dry. Some suggest spraying the barn with disinfectant regularly. I don't suggest this, either. If you simply keep the barn clean, nature can organically keep a good balance.

5. Goats require only minimum supplies. With the exception of the goat and the pen, you probably now have everything you need to keep goats. Old buckets or kitchen utensils can be used for feed and water. However, a few supplies make life easier.

Choose a veterinary guide book to give information.

Sticky, nontoxic fly strips will help control flying insects. They can be purchased at feed or hardware stores.

A knife works okay for trimming hooves, but it's best to invest a couple of dollars in a small pair of enders, such as are used on horses' hooves. I have the scar to prove that knives can be dangerous, and slower besides.

Hoegger Supply Company in Milford, Pennsylvania, has all sorts of goat equipment, including goat coats to keep them warm and dry in winter. I've heard that goat coats conserve enough body heat and energy in cold weather to keep milk production up during the cold weather drop.

Hardware, feed, and drugstore veterinary counters can help outfit you with the few items you may desire. The big mail-order catalogs have lots to offer, also.

American Supply House of Columbia, Missouri, has, among their other offerings, an herbal deworming compound and some good instruction booklets about goats and milk.

But most items you need can be found around the house.

ACQUIRING A GOAT

Before buying a goat, be sure to check local zoning laws. In some areas horses are allowed but goats are not. This class prejudice favoring high-cost pleasure animals above working animals makes me angry. Although I love horses, goats are less hassle, are more productive, and create less smell. I think priorities like these must change in our "civilized" society.

Goats can be acquired either as kids or full grown. In any case, it's best to buy from someone you know, if possible. Animals at auctions are sometimes sold because they have defective health or behavior.

Among authorities, male goats are called "bucks" and females are called "does." There are several common breeds available, some being more common in one region than others. My goats are a Nubian-Toggenberg cross, with the Nubian portion prevalent. They are excellent milk producers and beautiful animals. Their appearance is very similar to that of deer, only smaller.

When buying goats, keep in mind the following points:

1. Kids. You'll have to wait at least a year for production. But there's the advantage of knowing what kind of care they've had during that year, and being able to give care that will build good adult health and temperament. Also, your knowledge and handling ability will grow as the kid grows.
2. Adults. Here you have instant productivity. But you will also inherit any bad habits and health problems that developed with the previous owner and environment.

3. Billies. You will want to consider carefully before buying a billy. Your nannies only need to be bred once a year, so his practical value is limited. However, that once-a-year occasion is certainly easier if you're not obliged to ride around the countryside looking for a billy with your nanny in heat in the back seat. I would say that if you have several nannies and sufficient space, it is worthwhile to keep a billy. If your space is limited and/or you have only one or two nannies, it is probably not worthwhile.

A billy can help earn his keep by offering stud service. He will be happy to oblige, but this is a nuisance unless you have an adequate pen just for him and lady visitors. Fees are generally $10 per service and up, depending on his pedigree. Fees can be charged per day or per nanny serviced.

In caring for a billy, there are four things that can be done about buck odor:

1. Wash between his horns (a special cleanser is available from goat-supply houses).
2. Cauterize the glands between the horns when he is a kid, either with a heated tool or with acid meant for that purpose.
3. Don't keep bucks; or,
4. Groove on their scent. They do!

Billies that are to be kept as draft or meat animals should probably be castrated early. This is because a billy's aggressiveness is strongly associated with his sexuality. A castrated billy will grow faster and larger and not have buck odor. Castrating can be done at home by following the surgical procedure in a veterinary book, or by having a veterinarian come out. However, the best, easiest, and least painful way is by Elastrator, a special tool used to apply a very thick, tight, rubber stricture. This cuts off all circulation to the testicles, causing them to wither and fall off within a few weeks. To avoid danger to the health of the animal, like gangrene, you must have the proper tool and the proper band. No substitutes here, please.

THE PRODUCTION CYCLE

The nannies are bred by the billy usually sometime between September and March. The gestation period is five months. If you have several nannies, some can be bred in the fall and some in the spring to provide continuous milk production.

Nannies are in heat every twenty-one days, during which time they twitch their tails a lot, may have a discharge, and seem a bit nervous or behave slightly differently than usual. If you have a billy, put him in the pen at this time with the nanny and they'll figure it out.

The presence of a billy seems to make the symptoms of the heat more pronounced. If you don't have a billy, there may be several false alarms before you get her to stud at the right time. Or if you're into the technology more than I am, the vet will artificially inseminate her. This gives the option of providing a fancy registered father (whom she won't have the opportunity of meeting).

Don't milk during the last two months of pregnancy, as the nannies need the minerals for their babies' growth. Usually milk production has decreased or nearly stopped by itself about this time. If not, simply quit milking or gradually milk less, cutting down to once a day, then every other day, then not at all.

Generally, each nanny bears one to three kids without difficulty. The day of the birth, the area underneath the backbone and forward from the tail will cave in, becoming hollow. About the same time, a thick, eventually bloody, mucuous discharge will begin. Labor is usually under two hours. If labor contractions go on for most of a day, or seem difficult or wrong to you, it is well to call a vet, or at least another goatkeeper with more experience. The nannies usually manage nicely by themselves. And the new kids are usually on their feet in an hour. They spend the next hour or so looking for the milk supply, doing splits on their unsteady legs, missing the udder by inches, and falling between their mother's legs. Finally they locate the target.

Nothing quite matches the beauty of a spring birth. Our goats usually kid about Easter time. The kids are beautiful, though uncoordinated. Their legs are as long as their bodies.

Try to arrange to have your goat bred so that birth occurs during mild weather. Otherwise, unless your barn is heated, be sure to get the newborns into the house, at least until they are completely dry.

Recently we had the experience of bottle-feeding newborn triplets orphaned in stormy weather, each of us cuddling and warming one kid in blankets in our warm dining room. Another time, during a stormy-weather birth, we brought the newborns inside to dry off and warm up, and allowed the frantic mother to come inside briefly, too.

The feeding of kids can be handled in one of several ways. You can take the kid away from the mother the first day, shortly after birth. Some people prefer this, as there is little objection from mother and kid, or at least any objection is brief. This will mean that you have to bottle-feed the kid(s) about every five hours. Also, you must milk the mother twice daily, or three times if you want to build up the milk supply. Up to a point, she'll make as much as you take away. It is best if you feed the mother's milk back to the kids, at least for the first week or two. Use pop bottles with lamb nipples. Construct a substitute udder to feed several kids at once by suspending the bottles with nipples poking out of holes in the bottom of a net grapefruit bag, like this:

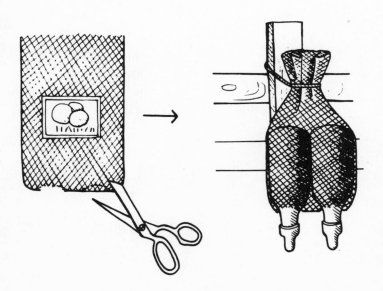

I strongly feel that mother's milk gives the kids the best start.

Some people prefer the above method, but I personally am not interested in being an omnipresent mother image for the kids, much as I like them. Early mother-care goes on day and night for a while, and that's a lot of commitment.

As an alternative method, leave the kid with the mother until it is about a week old. Then separate it from the mother during the daytime for another three days, feeding by bottle or bowl during the day. At ten days old, separate it entirely from the mother, feeding by bottle and/or bowl.

The kids and the mother become more attached to each other daily. If you wait until they are three or four weeks old to wean, the kids will remember and nurse any chance they get for a long time. If you are selling the kids while young, it won't matter much, as they can be gone at six weeks. But if you are planning to keep the kids, see that they are weaned properly from their mother as early as possible.

We have had good luck bowl-feeding kids at a week or less. You have to push their noses into the milk several times before they get the idea.

Kids can be fed one of the following or a combination of these: their mother's milk, regular instant powdered milk, or a calf-starter milk substitute. I feel the instant powdered milk, such as you get at the grocery, is just not complete enough. If I use it, and I have used it after the kids were well-started, I mix it stronger than suggested, adding also 1 cup goat's whole milk, 1 teaspoon molasses, and 1 teaspoon soy oil per quart of liquid as a supplement. Calf-starter milk substitute is formulated especially for young animals, but I object to the chemicals, including antibiotics, that are frequently part of the ration. I think new kids should get their mother's milk, which is perfectly formulated for them and contains natural antibodies besides.

About the third day I usually begin to milk the mother once a day for our own use, in addition to the kids' nursing. This will increase milk production and help guard against mastitis, a disease of the udder which is aggravated if the udder is not properly emptied. Sometimes the kids will favor one teat so the udder doesn't get properly emptied. Milk from a goat with mastitis should be thrown away.

Kids begin to sample hay when only a few days old—if they have access to it. They will eat a little grain (calf ration, if you like) at ten days to two weeks. Gradually increase both, and see that they have water and salt. They must also be kept dry and reasonably warm, something else the mother will do for them if you leave them with her for the first few days.

If you wish to dehorn the kids, this is best done at three to five days, either with heat or the proper acid. According to myth, nannies have no horns and billies have horns. Not so. Horns are a genetically related characteristic. We've had both horned nannies and hornless billies. It just depends on the genetic background of the parents. Goats' horns are good protection against marauding animals. Nannies' horns are not very large, but the horns of billies can be downright dangerous.

HOW TO MILK

To milk animals, take the top of the teat between thumb and forefinger. Squeeze from the top of the teat downward in a rhythmic motion, allowing the squeezing motion to move like a wave from forefinger to third, fourth, and fifth finger. By squeezing, the thumb and forefinger act as a valve, shutting off milk from the udder and forcing the milk out of the teat. Releasing admits more milk to the teat. It's easy with practice. And are my hands and forearms strong!

Strain and refrigerate the milk immediately. Clean the milking bucket and storage jars with hot water and soap and preferably sterilize them. Further directions for care and use of milk are found under the dairy section.

For milking less than a gallon, I find a party-size drip coffee pot works very well. The part I use is the gallon-size pitcher, the strainer insert that fits into the top of the pitcher, and the lid. Coffee filters fit right inside. This prevents most dirt falling into the milk in the first place, although I strain again into the jars. The whole unit can be heated directly over the stove burner to sterilize.

Goats' milk is naturally homogenized, and the tiny fat globules are spread throughout the milk. So if you wish to separate the milk from the cream, you must use a mechanical separator. Some cream will rise to the top in a day or two. You can pour that off daily into a separate jar. But you probably won't get enough this way to whip or to make butter.

A small separator can be purchased from Hoegger Supply Company for under $150 (See *Directory of Sources*). However, you may be able to locate a good used separator for under $25 if you look around. Parts are hard to find, so be sure all are there. Almost all used models will need a new "O" ring, to be purchased from a dairy supply house. We acquired a used Royal Blue table model made by Ward's circa 1940. It works fine now, but we spent lots of time finding and making a couple of parts.

I don't pasteurize the milk from our goats because I know they are healthy and because pasteurization destroys some nutrients.

Goats are healthy animals in general. They need no inoculations or testing, unless you want to sell the milk for human consumption, which requires licensing.

The most common health problem of goats is bloat, caused by overeating grain or green hay. This is not likely to occur in goats who are confined, as they depend on you for feed. Bloat causes their left side to puff out. Ordinary bloat can be eased by massaging the stomach at the bulge. Keep the goat on its feet, offer all the tree bark it wants, and give bicarbonate of soda, a spoonful at a time. Goats can handle simple bloat themselves if they have access to bark and a soda lick.

You can get an idea of the seriousness of the bloat by the condition of the animals. If they look like you feel after Thanksgiving dinner, it is minor. If they look sick, it is serious.

Serious bloat, which can cause death, must be alleviated immediately by an incision or a puncture directly into the bulge in the stomach where gas has accumulated, on the goat's left side. This can be done with a knife, an ice pick, or a special hollow needle which attaches to bloat medication to inject into the stomach. This will release the gas without harm. These procedures can be found in veterinary guide books. Bloat treatment should be kept on hand. See your drugstore's veterinary supply department.

Any other health problems definitely require personal familiarity and the help of a veterinarian. When it is necessary to call a vet, and we have found it infrequent, ask him all the questions you can. Most vets are happy to teach you about caring for your livestock. Ours has taught us some special procedures, including giving injections, and how to know when we need him. He has helped us much by phone, saving costs. Most towns and cities have a drugstore where veterinary supplies are available. Look in the Yellow Pages. After you learn symptoms and procedures for common problems, medicines and supplies can be obtained at the drugstore at low cost.

But all in all, goats are little fuss as long as you care for them faithfully. Feed them twice daily, milk them regularly, give them water and your love. In exchange, they offer their affection, entertainment, and that cold jug of fresh, whole milk always at hand in your refrigerator.

Rabbits

Rabbits are an extremely efficient source of meat, producing a great amount of meat in proportion to the cost of feed. But they're so cute, you say. Yes, but affection for the Easter Bunny has kept us from seeing their potential as food. After all, rabbit meat costs much less to raise than chicken meat, yet tastes much the same. (Rabbit costs much more in a grocery store.) And their skins make such nice mittens and coats. Just imagine the luxury of a blanket made of rabbit fur!

My friend Jon Glazer has been raising rabbits for four years, and he has given me the following advice.

SELECTION AND HEREDITY

In choosing rabbits to raise and breed, it is important to select them carefully. The basic genetic factors that a small rabbit breeder is concerned with are:

1. General health. Rabbits should not get sick easily. They should have bright, clear eyes. The ears and feet should be clean and healthy; so should their noses and rears.

2. Meatiness. They should have a blocky, chunky build, rather than a long, lean body. This means more meat.

3. Size and regularity of litters. Their litters should be of an even size, six to eight minimum. Rabbits for your hutches should not come from regularly small litters. Rabbits should weigh three and a half pounds minimum at two months. Don't choose runts.

4. Thickness of foot hair. Their feet should have thick, dense hair on the bottoms. This gives a high resistance to sore feet, an energy-draining affliction.

5. Quality of pelt. If you are going to use the pelts, they should be even and rich, with no bare or thin spots. White pelts bring up to twice the price of colored pelts on the professional market because they can be dyed. Colored pelts are preferred in the crafts market.

HANDLING

Don't lift rabbits by the ears. Use the scruff of the neck, like lifting a cat. Use your other hand to add some support under the haunches of a heavy rabbit. Watch out for those hind claws! When moving rabbits in and out of their cages, take care that their toes don't catch in the wire mesh at the door threshold.

CAGES

To raise rabbits well, build good cages. Do not use chicken wire for the floor—the rabbits' feet will get sore and cut. Wooden floors will absorb urine and cannot be cleaned. Build cages of welded wire mesh. The wires are welded together at their cross points, rather than being woven. The pieces are held together with J-clips. This mesh is very easy to clean, can be sterilized with a hand torch, and is very strong.

Jon builds his cages twelve feet long with four compartments per unit. The cages should be a minimum of eighteen inches high. Rabbits like to stand up. A depth of two feet and a three-or four-foot width is good. You should be able to reach in and pick up the rabbit wherever he is.

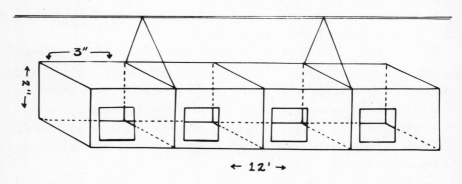

Hutches can be set on legs or sawhorses, but it works best to hang them, using baling wire or window-sash chain. Outdoors, a cable stretched between two trees will do nicely, as these cages are very strong. Rabbits can handle severe cold without much discomfort if they are dry and out of the wind. However, being burrowers, they are not suited to excesses of direct sunlight and heat over 80°. Oddly enough, they don't seem to mind swinging cages!

Put the cages in a well-lit but shady spot for indirect lighting. Improvise a rain and snow shield of plastic or canvas. It should not touch the cages because rabbits will gnaw it to shreds if they can. A wind screen of bamboo or vines on a lathe wall may be needed, depending on your location. If temperatures get too

high, you'll have to enclose your cages in a ventilated building and put sprinklers on the roof for air conditioning.

If you just can't afford to build cages or have to make temporary arrangements, contact the nearest airport to see if you can obtain some used air transport kennels. They are used just once and, if you can get some, are probably free.

SANITATION

Every so often, remove the rabbits and scrub or burn off the hair on the cage floor. Scrub the whole cage with soapy water and a disinfectant like Lysol or carbolic acid. Rinse the cage and let it dry.

Shovel out the manure whenever it gets unsanitary. The soil under the cages should be loose and absorbent. Earthworms grow well in the manure. Rabbit manure is an excellent fertilizer, and it does not need to age before being used.

Never use cement or wood under the cages because they are both impossible to clean. Well-drained soil is always best. Walkways surrounding the cages should be of wheelbarrow width and can be removable wooden pallets.

FEED AND WATER

Rabbits can be fed fresh vegetables, dry hay, or pelletized food. Fresh vegetables are often free, as your local supermarket discards spoiled or unsightly (and therefore unsalable) vegetables daily. Ask the produce manager. Rabbits cannot live on lettuce alone; they need about 15 percent protein. You will have to supplement the vegetables with protein hay, such as alfalfa or clover.

If you feed bulky, loose food, you will spend a lot of daily energy cleaning cages. Pelletized feed works best because it is neat and compact, and pellets with a variety of ingredients are generally better nutritionally. Galvanized feed hoppers that attach to the cages can be bought for little or improvised from rectangular metal cans.

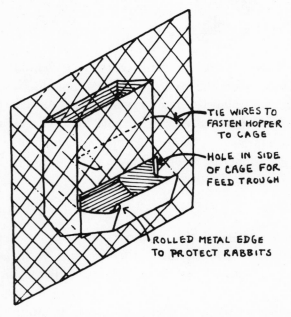

TIE WIRES TO FASTEN HOPPER TO CAGE

HOLE IN SIDE OF CAGE FOR FEED TROUGH

ROLLED METAL EDGE TO PROTECT RABBITS

The bulk of the hopper goes outside the cage. The feed trough portion goes through a cut opening.

Each individual compartment should have a spool of salt hung from a wire at the top of the cage. Hang it away from the feed and water so that your rabbits' ears don't continually rub on it.

Rabbits drink lots of water. A doe and her litter can use a

gallon a day in the summer. Best is an automatic water system. When a rabbit licks the tip, it momentarily releases a dribble.

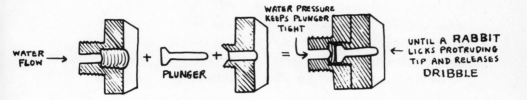

Systems such as this can work during very cold weather if special heater cable is installed in the pipe (not outside, because the rabbits will gnaw it).

If you have no electricity, or cannot afford special heating equipment, use a coffee or tobacco can in freezing weather. Wide cans that are not very deep are preferred, as bunnies can fall in and drown if they can't climb out. You'll have to improvise a fastener so the doe can't lift and dump the can. Ice will break ceramic water dishes. Crocks and cans are a poor choice compared to automatic systems because they have inadequate capacity and get funky with food crumbs and droppings. Also, a doe will nurse mostly at night and needs round-the-clock water.

RECORDS

Keep records to get the overall picture and to operate efficiently. Rabbit record cards are often free from feed dealers.

HUTCH RECORD CARD

Doe _____ Ear Tatto No. _____ Breed _____ Normal Weight _____

No. Nipples _____ Born _____ Sire _____ Dam _____

BUCK	Date of Service	Pregnancy Check	Date Kindled	Number of Young		At 8 weeks		REMARKS
				Kindled	Left	No. Left	Weight	

Records show parentage and continuity of desirable genes. Health is often reflected in weight, though a nursing doe often does lose weight naturally.

Records show trends. Thus, if a doe often has fourteen bunnies of which only five live, you shouldn't keep her for breeding. If at eight weeks the litter weighs under three pounds each, and you can't improve this by changing the feed, the buck or doe is poor. Likewise, the buck's card reflects his health and virility.

Perhaps a doe has a litter early, on the cage floor, and eats some. Is it a tendency or an incident? Perhaps the nest box had rain in it. All this information goes under remarks. Keep records faithfully; your rabbits will prosper and your yield will increase.

BREEDING

The buck is half your herd; don't neglect him. Bucks and does are good breeders for about two years, then diminish in value. Watch the record cards and start breeding replacements when indications are that production is dropping.

When a doe's productivity drops for three litters consecutively, it's time to replace her. Since a doe must be four to six months old to breed, remember this when selecting a bunny to replace her. Same with bucks.

A doe in heat will frequently rub her chin on things and rest with tail and haunches high. Take her to the buck. If you take the buck to her cage, she will fight him. The doe is not bred until the buck's hind feet slip forward, he hangs onto the doe, falls over sideways, and then dismounts. Leave the doe with the buck until they breed again. Then mark the date and other information on both the doe's and buck's information cards. On a calendar find the identical date the next month, count back three days inclusive, and mark that date as the day to give the doe a nest box.

GESTATION

A doe gestates for thirty to thirty-one days and needs the nest box three days before. Too soon and she may foul the nest; too late, and she may reject it. During the last week, put a small handful of Alber's Calf Manna on top of her feed daily to increase her milk and minimize nest-box deaths. Make sure she has plenty of clean water. Fasten the nest box so it won't tip.

NEST BOX

The box should be about ten inches high and a few inches wider and longer than the doe at rest. Fill the box with loose, fine, clean straw (not hay), packing material, or shredded newspaper. She will line it with fur from her belly.

A day after the litter is kindled (born), remove the nest gently from the cage. Carefully separate the fluff and count the living and dead. Mark the count on the doe's record card. You may want to discard the runts if there are over eight in the litter, unless the doe is good at raising large litters. If does kindle within three days of each other, bunnies can be crossadopted within those days to fill out a small litter or thin a large one. Contrary to rumor, does do not generally reject a litter that has been handled.

Check the litters once a week for dead bunnies.

BUNNIES AND THEIR MOMMIES

At about three weeks, when the bunnies start leaving the nest, remove and clean the box. Sterilize it with sun, fire, or carbolic acid and store it.

During the first three weeks continue feeding the doe a small handful of Calf Manna daily. During that time she will nurse only at night. At about three weeks, the bunnies will begin to eat feed. Discontinue the Manna at the end of the fourth week. At eight weeks, count and weigh the bunnies and enter the information on the record cards. Put the bunnies into a separate cage or butcher them. *Don't get chummy with your meat.* Separate the sexes by the time they are three months old to avoid unregulated breeding.

BUTCHERING AND COOKING

Those of you who homestead may be raising and processing your own meat. For some, the prospects of killing and butchering an animal are saddening or frightening. Yet if you are a meateater, it is well to come to grips with acquiring meat.

I find it interesting that some people make a clear-cut distinction between eating vegetable and animal life. I respect that decision, but having worked for years with both plants and animals, I feel strongly that plants respond to warmth and attention just as animals do. It is hard to say what the nature of vegetable consciousness might be. When I uproot or pluck a plant I wonder about this, yet am grateful. However, I do find it easier to take a plant life than an animal life.

Throughout all nature, life lives by consuming other life. I think it is well to understand that. Perhaps we should do as the Native Americans have customarily done—give thanks to the life which is about to become one with us, and acknowledge that we, too, one day will provide food for other organisms.

On the practical side of things, if you are a meateater it is well to raise animals for food. Meat, like everything else offered packaged today, is not as good as it should be. The animal offered at the meat counter most likely led a crowded, miserable life in confinement with other creatures who were to be slaughtered. They were probably filled with many chemicals during the course of their lives to make them more "marketable" faster.

On your little homestead, you will see a natural flow about

meateating if you keep animals. If you raise goats, you will soon realize that each spring fifty percent of your kids are bucks, and it is foolish to keep more than one for stud. If you raise rabbits, you are probably raising them only for the meat. If you raise chickens, there will be extra roosters who offer practical food. Extra roosters will lower egg-laying, consume expensive food, and crow raucously and continuously. They'll help interest you in eating them.

One hint I must offer—*never name a meat animal,* unless you name it "Delicious," "Yummy," "Dinner," or something similar. That way, when the day comes you can say, "Isn't this Delicious?" rather than "Isn't this Tommy?"

Our first experience with eating one of our animals evolved naturally. One day we arrived home to discover a doe goat had jumped the fence, gotten into the grain, overeaten, bloated, and just died. It was a cold, snowy December day. We knew she had just died, and we knew why. It seemed ridiculous, wasteful, and wrong to dig through frozen earth to bury her. We felt the right thing was to butcher her. So we did, quickly. We had to wait a few days for aging and to get beyond our emotional attachment before we were able to eat the meat, but the meat was delicious, like top sirloin, and it seemed that eating it was proper in the scheme of things.

We were careful to immediately gut the bloated goat. Then we carefully cleansed the inside with several batches of fresh snow.

Generally, if an animal has died suddenly from injury, it is okay to eat the meat. Depending on the injury, you may dispose of the injured area. A deer that has been hit by a car may be eaten if butchered promptly and if permission is gotten from game or law-enforcement people. But it is essential never to eat an animal that died of unknown causes or sickness, or that has been dead a while.

The killing and butchering processes below are as described to me by my friend Jon Glazer. He has been processing his own domestic and wild meat for some time. After living most of his life in New York City, he moved to a Western homestead several years ago.

The instructions are essentially similar for all grazers and most carnivores. From a home butcher's point of view, a rabbit, a goat, and a cow are not very different. Variations crop up due to size and meat distribution. A rabbit doesn't get jointed at elbows, knees, and pelvis because it is too small. A cow has an enormous backstrap, allowing a different variety of steak cuts. These instructions are specifically written with goats in mind, but are fine for all grazers, including deer.

Goats

The simplest way to kill a small to medium-sized animal is with a .22 rifle or pistol. If you calm the animal or treat it casually, you can put the muzzle of the gun almost up against it. Fire sideways, an inch below the base of an ear. The bullet is likely to exit on the other side, so be sure everything is clear in that direction. Or shoot against the back of the head, by its neck, so the bullet exits between the eyes. Or shoot between the eyes so the bullet hits around the spine.

Lacking a gun, or preferring not to use one, you can slit the animal's throat with a very sharp knife. If the animal is medium-sized or larger, the animal must be restrained. If the animal is small, like a goat kid, you may simply hold it on its side, pull the head back as far as you can, and cut the throat.

But the knife *must* be extremely sharp. You *must* be an accurate shot with the gun. You want to be absolutely sure that the animal dies immediately and doesn't suffer because you are squeamish, unsure, or scared.

These methods work for goats, deer, most grazing animals, and many carnivores. A larger caliber rifle should be used for larger animals. Pigs and cattle require a heavier caliber rifle because of thicker skull-bone structure. If you are going to cut up the animal within an hour or two of killing it, bleeding it is unnecessary. For longer periods, cut its throat and gut it immediately to preserve the taste and prop the rib cage open to cool the carcass.

If not butchered right away, the carcass *must be kept cool—under 40°.*

In hot weather, you must work quickly. When it's hot, all old meat is bad meat.

HOW TO BUTCHER A GOAT WITH A HEAVY SHEATH KNIFE

Get a big container for guts and another for organs to be saved. Have a pot of water or a hose handy. Sharpen your knife before beginning.

1. Rig a gambrel (also called a singletree).

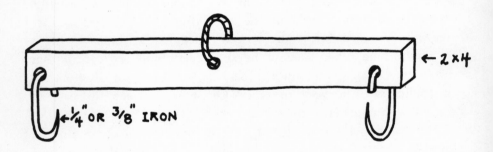

The hoisting loop can be made of rope. Hooks of 1/4- or 3/8-inch iron rod, sharpened, are free to swing sideways.

The hooks should be far enough apart to spread the goat's hind legs widely. If the hooks are too far apart, extend them with loops of coat hanger.

2. Hang a block and tackle, or at least a rope and pulley, from a beam or branch, rather high up. Figure what you'll tie the rope to after hoisting. (If the animal being butchered is heavy, the rope may be attached to a motor vehicle, which is then pulled forward a little to raise the animal.) Fasten the singletree to the hoist.

3. Cut crosswise through each hind leg, between the big Achilles tendon (which goes to the heel) and the bone. Put the hooks through these cuts.

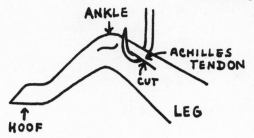

4. Hoist the animal until its head clears the ground. Secure the rope. Cut the head off. Cut all around the bone, and twist. The vertebrae will separate. Don't saw bone with your knife; it does no good.

5. Cut off the front feet at the ankle. This takes some experience. There's a double joint. Cut all around the one nearest the body, through skin and gristle. Find the joints by feeling with your fingers. Flex the joints. After cutting, break foot backwards, using hard pressure. Cut any remaining tendons.

6. Cut the skin all around the hind legs at the tendon cuts. *Don't* cut the tendons. From these cuts, slit the skin down the inside of the legs to the crotch.

7. Stand behind the carcass. Use your knife as needed to work the skin toward you and over the haunches. If you are interested in tanning the skin, be careful not to cut it, and leave all the flesh on the carcass.

8. Work the skin down the legs as needed to loosen it at the haunches. After the skin is started, you can often strip it off like a sock by pulling very hard. In all skinning, there are places where you can work a thumb, finger, or fist between skin and flesh with a rolling motion. This is better and faster than using a knife. Goat skin adheres tightly, deer more loosely, rabbit very loosely.

9. Work the skin down the haunches around the rectum and tail. Circle the rectum with your fingers and free it from the tail. Cut it free of the skin. Use your knife carefully and vertically to free the rectum from the muscle it passes through, cutting meat where necessary. Pull the rectum up enough to knot it. Tie a knot in it and let it drop into the body.

10. Cut the tail off. All vertebrae have soft cartilage between them. Cut at the high spots. Start in with the point of the knife.

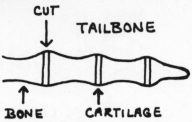

11. You can now, with effort, strip the entire skin off like a tube. It will turn inside out as it comes off. Very hard pulling and minimal cutting works best. You can also slit the belly skin. Do this slowly and carefully so as not to cut the belly muscles.

12. Put the skin aside. Put the gut bucket under the animal where the guts can fall into it. Cut the belly muscle at the crotch. Put two fingers down into the cut, pulling the muscle away from the guts. Put your knife point down, edge out, between your fingers. Your fingers will prevent the point from piercing the guts. Slit down to the breastbone.

Let the guts drop into the bucket. With your hands, strip the leaf fat off the intestines (whitish lacy-looking stuff) and save it for lard. Save the kidneys. They are against the back of the cavity near the spine—egg-sized and bean-shaped, nested in fat.

13. Reach behind the large stomach, first with your free hand and then with your knife. Cut the stomach free as far toward the head as possible. *Don't* cut the stomach. Cut the esophagus.

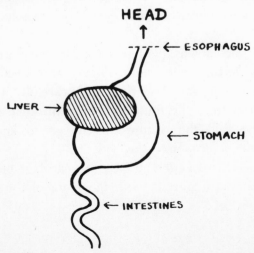

14. Roll the stomach and liver into the gut bucket. Using your fingers only, separate liver from stomach until the only points of attachment are some large blood vessels. Cut these. Turn the liver over. Examine the folds. If you find an elongated bladder, full or empty, remove it very gently with a knife. *Don't* cut it. This is the gall bladder, full of bitter bile. It is missing in most deer, but present in rabbits. Always look for it.

15. If you did cut the guts or gall bladder, wash all contaminated meat *immediately* and *thoroughly* with *lots* of cold water.

16. Hold your knife in both hands, point and edge down. Cut down the breastbone, centered or off along an edge. Push very hard. You may have to chop with the knife, and a small ax is handy here. This process is called "grolloching" (grolloking).

17. The heart lies in a sheath against the breastbone between the big pinkish lungs. In a goat it is about fist-sized and purple-brown. Cut if off at the ventricles where it gets complicated.

18. Dogs and cats like the lungs. Or they can go in the ground-meat mixture.

This completes the skinning and gutting. Remove the gut bucket and organ pot. Cover them to ward off flies, cats, and dogs. Hose or wash down the entire cavity and your knife and hands.

Take five.

19. Get a large container with a cover for limbs and parts. Cut between each shoulder blade and the ribs, spreading the front leg away from the body to make this easier. There is no joint, and each front leg will come off easily.

20. Look inside the rib cage. Locate the ribs furthest from the neck. Feel the spinal vertebrae. Find the high point just past the last rib juncture, going toward the tail. Put the point of your knife in the high spot, into the gristle. Hold it horizontally and wiggle it from side to side till the gristle is mostly cut.

21. Lay the knife on top of the rib, on its side. Stab through all the way and slice outward. Do this in both directions so that the spine alone connects the upper and lower body parts.

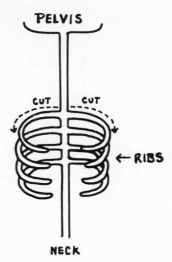

22. Walk behind the carcass and grab its neck. Pull up and back to further break the joint you've been cutting. After the bones are separated, finish the cut with a knife.

The rib cage has been suspended by the spine. When it comes free, it will be a sudden, dropping weight. Be prepared for this. Don't drop it. You can cut a finger-hold between a couple of ribs.

23. Unhook one hind leg from the gambrel. Use the knife, front and back, to cut the meat from the pelvis. Let the knife follow and feel the bone. A horizontal line drawn through the arch of the pubis will intersect the ball-and-socket joint of thigh bone and hip bone.

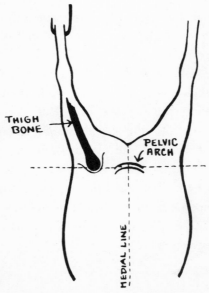

24. Pull the leg outward when this joint is exposed. Work the point of the knife into the socket to cut the ligament there. Cut around the socket until the joint falls free. Finish severing the leg, following the curve of the hip bone. Don't drop it as it comes free.

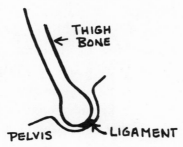

25. Cut the pelvis and spine section free of the remaining leg, as in **23** and **24**.

26. Unhook and take down the remaining leg. Use an ax to chop off the feet, if you like. There are foot joints a knife can find, but they are complex and not obvious.

This completes the dismembering. Take all sections to a work table.

27. Put a front leg on the table. Feel and flex the joint between shoulder blade and upper leg. This is a simple joint. Cut the meat and expose this joint and sever it.

Always let your knife follow the bone. Slip it between bones at joints.

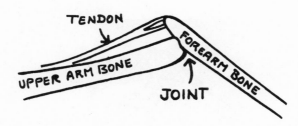

28. If you have a long, thin knife, use it as well as the sheath knife from here on. These cuts can be done with a one-inch penknife, too, though not as smoothly.

29. There is a ridge on one side of the shoulder blade. Cut down along either side of it. Turn the blade flat and cut horizontally along the shoulder blade both ways from the ridge to the edge. This yields two nice meaty chunks. For little steaks, cut these accross the muscle grain.

Turn the bone over. Slice off the thin meat there. It can be fried or grilled in chunks, or ground. It is tender.

30. Sever the upper arm from the forearm. This joint goes as indicated in the illustration. Feel it out as you go.

31. Locate the place where flesh lies thinnest over the upper arm bone. Cut to the bone, along it, and around it. Remove this meat in one piece. Fold it back into shape without the bone and cut it crosswise for steaks.

If you have a meat saw (a very coarse-toothed hacksaw is okay), you can cut the upper arm, bone and all.

32. Pare the meat off the forearm. This is gristly, good only for grinding or for stews.

33. For the rib cage use a knife and hammer, or an ax, to cut off the ribs about halfway, cutting against a block. The meat off these strips can be ground, jerked, or stewed. Chop off the neck. Use it for stew or section it with the ax for bony steaks.

34. If you can split the spine with an ax or saw, you can then separate the ribs into groups of two or three for spareribs.

35. If you have neither an ax nor a saw, you can remove the backstrap in two long strips. This is very tender meat.

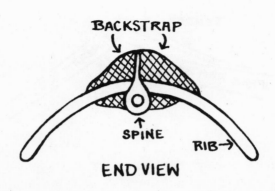

36. Note that the backstrap has a shiny, tough sheath mostly on one face. Lay this face on the cutting board. Slice off 2- or 3-inch chunks. Cut each chunk in half down to the gristle, so you can open the piece like a butterfly. These are butterfly steaks. Grind or jerk the rest of the rib meat. Clear off the soup bones.

37. Lay the pelvis-spine on the table. Remove the backstrap similarly. This section has meat on the underside, too. Sever the spine through a cartilage disk. (Yep, that's what slips out of place!)

38. Pare the rest of the meat off the pelvis. There should be little, all in irregular scraps. Use it for ground meat.

39. Clear the table. Get a hind leg. Tuck the ankle between your arm and side as you are holding the knee up and looking at it. There is a whitish band of ligament at the knee. Rest your knife across the knee, blade toward you. Cut down into the ligament, letting your knife follow the curve of the knuckle at the end of the upper leg bone. This knuckle is under the ligament. Undercut the joint as well, and separate.

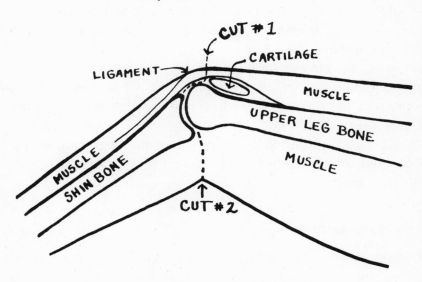

40. All the meat on the shin bone is for stewing or grinding. Let your knife point follow the bone curves, and the meat comes off easily.

41. Here the long knife is handy. Hold the thigh with the cartilage side up and nearest you. (Same orientation as in **39**.) Use a pointed knife to cut the meat alongside the cartilage on both sides, enough so you can lift the cartilage.

42. Hold the long knife horizontal, blade away from you. Slip it under the cartilage. Following the length of the bone, cut and lift off a big chunk.

43. Use the sheath knife. Cut along and around the bone. Remove the remaining meat.

44. These chunks cut across give big steaks. All round bones when cracked make good soup.

45. If you like brains, peel the skin from the top of the head. Then, if you have a hacksaw or an ax, cut off the top of the head. Brains are good scrambled with eggs and are very nutritious.

46. Wash clotted blood out of the heart. Cut it into sections. Fry with garlic and butter.

47. Cut the liver into three or four chunks and wash it. Massage in cold water to get the excess blood out. It is best cooked until there is only a faint tinge of pink. Overcooked liver is dry and has poor texture.

48. Slice the kidneys open and use a small scissors to remove most of the white matter. Soak them in white vinegar for an hour and they'll taste fine when cooked. They're best fried in a little beer.

49. Clean up, giving all waste to scavenging dogs, cats, or pigs. Bears and coyotes like guts, too—something to remember.

50. Bon appétit!

Miscellaneous hints

The convenience of a meat saw, which costs five to ten dollars, allows you to section bones wherever desired. However, you may find it more convenient to bone the meat, which requires only a knife and allows more freezer space. A heavy Cutco kitchen shears (about ten dollars) can be used more easily than a knife on poultry and small animals.

The same basic directions can be used for butchering hogs. However, the skin is used for cracklings, the fat for lard, the head for head cheese, and the hooves for pickled knuckles. Hogs are usually scalded and dehaired first. Much time and effort can be saved by simply skinning them as instructed here.

Birds can be cut through the ribs, separating back and breast.

A goat may be hung by its neck, or a deer by its antlers. In that case, the skin *must* be slit from throat to crotch, and out from this cut to ankles and wrists. Skinning starts at the neck. The chest skin and neck skin require a knife. The back, sides, and legs only need fist and fingers. The belly cut starts at the navel and goes first down, then up. Guts drop out rather neatly. Grolloching proceeds upward. Otherwise, everything is the same.

Your work will become better as you develop your sense of touch and feel. Flex joints. Take them apart with a penknife and see how they fit.

Keep your knife sharp.

When skinning, avoid getting hair on the meat. Rinse your knife and hands occasionally.

ROAST GOAT WITH BARBECUE SAUCE

Preheat oven to 450º. Sprinkle the **meat (about 5 pounds)** with **salt and pepper**. Place the pieces in a large roasting pan. Cover and bake two hours, stirring from time to time, but never adding liquid. For the sauce, sauté in **3 tablespoons vegetable oil**:

2 cups onions, chopped
1-1/2 cups green pepper, chopped
3 cloves garlic, chopped

1 teaspoon crushed peppercorns
1 teaspoon fresh cumin seeds

Add **1 pound tomatoes, chopped**. Simmer together five minutes, then spread on the meat. Reduce heat to 350º and roast another hour. Then serve. Serves 10 to 12.

MARILYNNE AND JOHN'S TERIYAKI

Cut into small thin steaks or strips **1 to 2 pounds goat, elk, or venison.** For one to three days, marinate (soak) meat in the refrigerator in the following sauce:

1/2 cup tamari sauce or soy sauce
1/4 cup white wine
1 to 2 cloves garlic, minced
2 tablespoons brown sugar
1/2 teaspoon ground ginger

Broil steaks or cook strips in a fondue pot. I first tasted elk teriyaki made like this on a recent New Year's Eve and promptly gave my friends, the cooks, my nonannual Best Recipe of the Year award! Serves 2 to 4.

EASY ROAST CHEVON

Chevon is the official name for goat meat. This simple method is a delicious way of preparing young goat.

Rub the meat with **salt, pepper,** and **a little garlic oil.**

Roast in a heavy pan in an oven set at 300°. Cooking time for 5 pounds of meat is 3 or 4 hours, depending on the meat, the altitude, and the oven. The meat is more tender and moist if the pan is covered; however, to avoid any "wild" taste, the meat can be kept uncovered.

OUTDOOR ROAST KID

Prepare a fire of hardwood or charcoal. When the coals are white-hot, put the kid on a spit and suspend over the fire, turning it frequently. Or cut in half, laying the two halves on a grill above the fire. Baste frequently with a mixture of:

2 cups tamari or soy sauce   **1/2 cup brown sugar**
1 cup white wine   **1 tablespoon ground ginger**
1 tablespoon garlic oil   **1 cup cooking oil**

Serve when brown outside, pink inside. It won't last long, especially if served in crisp mountain air on a spring day.

Chickens

For chickens (and other fowl), first catch the bird. Take it off its roost after dusk or before dawn when it is quiescent. It's best to fast the creature for twelve hours.

Chickens may be killed by decapitating with a sharp ax or knife. The bird's neck may be stretched and confined by placing it on a board into which two nails have been driven at angles to hold the neck steady. Hold or tie the wings to prevent flapping. Or if someone is there to help you, lay the chicken on its side on the board, with you holding the wings and someone else gently pressing a light board over the head to hold the head steady and prevent the chicken from seeing. The object is to kill the chicken as quickly and painlessly as possible; both the chicken's body and your hand must be steady.

Or the bird's throat may be cut, cutting both the large vein and the cross vein to insure good bleeding, as illustrated below. This may be done while the bird is hung by the feet, which allows free bleeding.

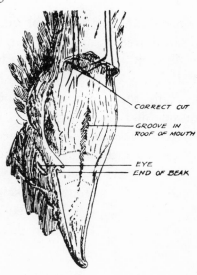

CORRECT CUT

GROOVE IN
ROOF OF MOUTH

EYE
END OF BEAK

After the bird stops bleeding and breathing, it should be scalded for 30 to 75 seconds in water at approximately 140° F. The exact time and temperature varies with the kind and age of the poultry. Scalding allows easier picking of the feathers from the bird. The large tail and wing feathers are pulled first. Then each bird should be examined carefully for pinfeathers, which may be removed by gripping the pinfeathers between the blade of a dull knife and the thumb. The remaining hairs should be singed with a burning match or candle, rapidly so the flesh isn't damaged.

To eviscerate the bird:

1. Cut off the head if you have not already done so.

2. Remove shanks by cutting through the large joint. (The shank is the area from the foot to the knee.)

3. Cut the skin on the back of the neck from where the head was severed to the base of the neck, then pull the skin down to the shoulder.

4. The gullet, crop, and windpipe are removed by pulling them away from the neck skin, then cutting them off at the point nearest to the entrance to the body cavity.

5. Cut the neck from the body at the beginning of the back.

6. Remove the oil sac, located on the back of the bird at the base of the tail. Cut under the sac to the backbone and up toward the tail.

7. Remove the entrails. Make a vertical cut below the end of the breastbone (keel) down to and around the vent (anus). The gizzard is pulled through the opening, together with the liver, heart, and intestinal tract. Be careful to avoid cutting the intestines and organs and spilling their contents. Remove the lungs. Then wash the carcass inside and out.

8. The gizzard, liver, and heart are removed from the viscera. Split the gizzard lengthwise through the thick muscle. The lining and contents are carefully peeled out, avoiding spillage.

9. Remove the gall bladder without breaking it by grasping it between the thumb and forefinger on one hand, close to the liver, holding the liver with the other hand, and pulling the gall bladder away.

10. Trim and wash the heart free of blood.
11. Chill immediately.

Birds can be skinned rather than plucked, if you prefer. If plucked, the feathers can be washed and dried in a net bag for use in pillowmaking.

FRIED CHICKEN

Select a tender young fryer. Heat a cast-iron skillet at medium heat. Add **2 cups cooking oil.**

Into a brown paper grocery bag, put the **cut-up chicken** and **2 cups whole-wheat flour, garlic powder, onion powder, black pepper, and salt.** Shake the bag until chicken is well coated. Arrange chicken in hot oil. Keep heat medium high until the chicken becomes golden brown. Then cover pan and turn to medium low. Simmer 30-45 minutes until tender and meat comes off bone easily. Put on paper to absorb oil, then serve. Serves 2 to 4, depending on the size of the chicken.

PINEAPPLE CURRIED CHICKEN

Either a young fryer or an older chicken will work well for this. Preheat oven to 300°. Arrange in layers in a casserole dish:

1 chicken, cut in pieces
1 cup mushrooms, sliced or whole
1/2 onion, chopped
2-1/2 cups brown rice, uncooked (if precooked, add less rice, more liquid)
1 pineapple cut into chunks, or 1 20-ounce can pineapple

Sprinkle with **1 clove garlic, chopped, 1 tablespoon curry powder,** and **1/4 teaspoon paprika.** Pour **1-1/2 cups unsweetened pineapple juice** over all. Cover casserole and bake 1-1/2 to 2 hours, until very tender. Serves 2 to 4, depending on the size of the chicken.

Rabbits

The easiest and most efficient way to kill two-to-three-month-old rabbits is to break their necks.

1. With your right hand, grasp the rabbit by the neck and lift it.
2. With your left hand, grab the rabbit's hind legs above the heels.
3. Smoothly lift the feet and lower the head.
4. Slide your right hand around so that your fingers are beneath the rabbit's chin and your thumb behind its neck.
5. Press down *hard* with your thumb while lifting the chin. Stretch the rabbit with your right thumb and left hand. *Hard.* This will dislocate the neck and break it. Larger rabbits have thick necks, hard to break. In this case, hit the rabbit hard across the back of its head, behind the ears, with a piece of pipe. The rabbit will twitch for a while, although dead. Continue with the butchering and tanning instructions.

Remember, the most humane way to kill meat is the fast, efficient way. The creature is giving its life energy to you; do not cause it to suffer unnecessarily. Cook with loving care.

COOKING

Use any chicken recipe, or one of the following:

JON'S STEWED RABBIT

Put **rabbit** into a stew pot with **lots of vegetables and seasoning to taste**. Cover scantily with **water**, enough to prevent sticking. Simmer covered until the meat begins to fall apart.

Fry **rice** in **butter**. Pour the stew over the rice. Cover and turn the flame way down. Cook until the rice is fluffed.

This recipe serves from 4 to 8, depending on the quantity of vegetables and rice you add. For example, you could use **1 potato,**

1 carrot, 1 stalk of celery, 1/3 onion, 1/2 cup uncooked rice per person. Improvise according to availability and what smells good together. Season with **basil** and **thyme.**

JON'S RABBIT CASSEROLE PAR EXCELLENCE

In a greased skillet fry **fine-cut potatoes** and an equal amount of **chopped onions** until brown and soft. Keep moist with **ketchup, Worchestershire, or soy sauce.** Add **a little garlic, wine vinegar, bay leaf,** and **rosemary.** Scrape it all to one side of the skillet and put in the **rabbit,** setting aside the organs. Cover the rabbit with the potato and onion mixture, and put a heavy cover on the skillet. Keep it moist.

Mix **diced apple, honey,** and **spices (curry, mustard, cumin, basil, oregano, salt, pepper).** Stir contents of skillet to prevent burning and add above mixture, plus **organs** and **a couple of beaten eggs.** Stir and cook covered until meat looks done throughout, then uncover and fry until golden brown. Serves 4 to 6. Very good!

COUNTRY LORE

Animal Products: Soap, Candles, and Tanning

Having butchered the animal, let nothing go to waste. The fat can be used to make soap and candles for your home. The skin should be tanned and used for clothing or moccasins.

HOMEMADE SOAP

Grandma could make 40 pounds of biodegradable soap with 12 pounds of fat and a barrel of wood ashes. You can make soap easily with fat and prepared lye.

Save and melt all animal fats as you accumulate them. Strain them into a clean, covered can; then they'll be ready at soapmaking time. Here's how:

Clean all fats by bringing to a boil in an equal amount of water. Remove from the heat and stir in 1 quart of cold water for each gallon of liquid. Remove fat from top when firm. Never use glass, stoneware, or aluminum pots for soapmaking. Do use stainless steel or unchipped enamel pots and wash them well before using for cooking.

To make 9 pounds of soap, slowly add **1 can lye** (from grocery store) to **2-1/2 pints cold water.** Stir with a wooden spoon or stick until dissolved. Melt **6 pounds of clean fat,** then let it cool to correct temperature (between 95° and 98°, or as shown on the lye can). Pour the warm lye solution (also 95° to 98°) into the melted fat in a thin, steady stream, stirring slowly and evenly. Too rapid pouring or stirring causes separation. Continue slow stirring for 10-20 minutes until mixture becomes the texture of thick honey.

Pour into a wooden or cardboard box lined with a damp cotton cloth. Cover with an old blanket or rug to retain the heat. Let stand 24 hours. Remove and cut bars and separate to dry. Let age 2 weeks. My mother always ground her soap in a meat grinder to make soap flakes.

HOMEMADE LYE

Outdoors, arrange a wooden container with holes in the bottom over a catch trough. Into the container (a wooden barrel works fine), place **a layer of straw** and **a couple of quarts of lime.** Then fill with **wood ashes,** or layer the ashes with **lime rock,** if no lime is available. Slowly pour **several pails of cold water** over this. Repeat, pouring the water over the mixture several times a day for several days. When the lye in the trough is deep red in color and can float an egg or a potato, it is ready. Use 3 pounds of fat to a 10-quart pail of strong lye for soapmaking.

EASY, HEATLESS SOAPMAKING

I found the following oldtime recommended formula in an 1866 book called *Dr. Chase's Recipes, or Information for Everybody.* This method allows the fat and lye to accumulate in one place, automatically making soap over a long period of time.

Put the fat into a cask as it accumulates, and add strong **homemade lye solution.** During the year, as the fat increases in the keg, stir in more strong lye, using a stick. When the cask is full, the soap will be ready. The only purpose of boiling in soapmaking is to increase the strength of weak lye and to hasten the process.

TALLOW CANDLES

Obtain candle wicking from a candle supply store if possible, letting the proprietor know what you plan, so he can supply the appropriate wicking. Otherwise, braid together several thicknesses of thick cotton store string to make the wicking.

Tie the wicks to a stick 3 inches apart. Dip the wicks repeatedly into a warm mixture of **rendered fat (tallow).** Dip until candles reach desired thickness. Wrap the finished candles in one layer of paper. Candles made with tallow alone don't burn as well and don't keep as well—especially in summer—as candles with beeswax added.

TALLOW-BEESWAX CANDLES

Melt together **tallow,** cleansed as in soapmaking, and **beeswax** in whatever quantities you have available. (The more beeswax, the more substantial the candle.) Dip or pour candles, as desired.

TANNING SKINS

1. Make tea for tanning. The tanning substance can be made either from oak bark boiled in a little water until very strong, or regular black tea boiled until strong (8-10 Lipton's family tea bags are fine).

2. Scrape all fat and flesh from the underside of the fresh skin.

3. Scrape off all hair, if desired.

4. Stretch skin on a board or on the side of a building and nail it down, underside out.

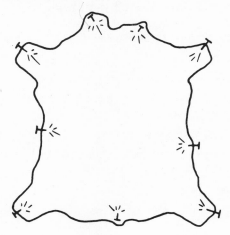

5. Pour or brush tanning tea onto the skin, saturating the skin.

6. Repeat step 5 every hour for 4 or 5 hours, keeping the skin moist with the tanning solution for 1 day.

7. The animal's brains rubbed in after the tanning solution will keep the skin pliable. Or use neetsfoot oil.

8. Allow the skin to partially dry, then while still damp remove from board.

9. To soften, hold one side of skin in each hand over a chair back or table edge. Rub back and forth repeatedly, allowing the blunt edge to break the fibers in the skin, thereby softening it.

10. Skins not to be tanned immediately should be heavily salted down, after scraping off the flesh. However, don't expect the same fine results from old skins as from fresh skins.

TABLES

Equivalents by Volume

(All Measurements Level)

1 quart	4 cups
1 cup	8 fluid ounces
	1/2 pint
	16 tablespoons
2 tablespoons	1 fluid ounce
1 tablespoon	3 teaspoons
1 pound regular butter or margarine	4 sticks
	2 cups
1 pound whipped butter or margarine	6 sticks
	2 8-ounce containers
	3 cups

One Ingredient for Another

For These	You May Use These
1 cup butter or margarine, for shortening	7/8 cup lard, or rendered fat, with 1/2 tsp. salt. Or 1 cup hydrogenated fat (cooking fat sold under brand name) with 1/2 tsp. salt.
1 square (1 oz.) chocolate	3 tbs. cocoa plus 1 tb. fat.
1 tsp. sulfate-phosphate baking powder	1-1/2 tsps. phosphate baking powder. Or 2 tsps. tartrate baking powder.
1 cup buttermilk or sour milk, for baking	1 cup sweet milk mixed with one of the following: 1 tb. vinegar. Or 1 tb. lemon juice. Or 1-3/4 tsps. cream of tartar.
1 cup fluid whole milk	1/2 cup evaporated milk plus 1/2 cup water. Or 1 cup reconstituted dry whole milk. Or 1 cup reconstituted nonfat dry milk plus 2-1/2 tsps. butter or margarine. (To reconstitute dry milk, follow directions on the package.)

SOURCE: "Family Fare," Home and Gardening Bulletin, No. 1, *U.S. Department of Agriculture.*

Food Preparation at High Altitudes

Boiling Temperatures of
Water at Various Altitudes

Altitude	Boiling point of water	
Sea level	212 º F.	100 º C.
2,000 ft.	208	98
5,000	203	95
7,500	199	92
10,000	195	90

Cake Recipe Adjustment Guide for High Altitudes

Adjustment	3,000 ft.	5,000 ft.	7,000 ft.
Reduce baking powder for each tsp., decrease	1/8 tsp.	1/8-1/4 tsp.	1/4 tsp.
Reduce sugar for each cup, decrease	0-1 tb.	0-2 tbs.	1-3 tbs.
Increase liquid for each cup, add	1-2 tbs.	2-4 tbs.	3-4 tbs.

Note: When two amounts are given, the smaller adjustment should be tried first; then, if cake still needs improvement, the larger adjustment can be used the next time.

In making very rich cakes at high altitudes, it is sometimes necessary to reduce shortening by 1 or 2 tablespoons. Recipes using soda may require a very slight reduction of this leavening. On the other hand, the amount of egg may be increased at highest altitudes. This has possibilities in recipe adjustments for angel food and sponge cakes.

SOURCE: "High Altitude Food Preparation," Pamphlet No. 41, *Colorado State University, Cooperative Extension Service.*

Measures and Temperatures

Common Food Measures

3 teaspoons	1 tablespoon
2 tablespoons	1 fluid ounce
4 tablespoons	1/4 cup
6 tablespoons	3/8 cup
8 tablespoons	1/2 cup
16 tablespoons	1 cup
1 cup	8 fluid ounces
2 cups	1 pint
2 pints	1 quart

Oven Temperatures

Very slow	250° and 275° F.
Slow	300° and 325° F.
Moderate	350° and 375° F.
Hot	400° and 425° F.
Very hot	450° and 475° F.
Extremely hot	500° and 525° F.

SOURCE: "Family Fare," Home and Gardening Bulletin, No. 1, *U.S. Department of Agriculture.*

DIRECTORY OF SOURCES

Mail-order sources for the tools and supplies suggested in this book:

BOOKS

Brillig Works Bookstore
1322 College
Boulder, Colorado 80302
   This established, cooperative bookstore is also developing an organic homestead.

Key Book Center
1720 15th Street
Boulder, Colorado 80302
   Titles concerning human development and practical processes. Any mail order filled. Catalog on request.

CHEESE- AND YOGURT-MAKING SUPPLIES

Christian Hansen's Laboratory, Inc.
9015 West Maple Street
Milwaukee, Wisconsin 53214
   Special yogurt cultures, such as *Lactobacillus acidophilus*, $3.75 each.

Springfield Creamery
145 North 3rd Street
Springfield, Oregon 97477
   Will answer inquiries about yogurt and yogurt-making supplies. Currently no mail orders filled, but this may change.

DAIRY GOAT EQUIPMENT

Hoegger Supply Company
Milford, Pennsylvania 18337
All equipment needed for goatkeeping, including cream separators.

FLOUR MILLS

Homestead Industries
2014 Los Angeles Avenue
Berkeley, California 94707
Electric stone flour mills $60 to $195. Bicycle-powered generators available.

Nelson & Sons
P. O. Box 1296
Salt Lake City, Utah 84110
Quaker flour mills.

R & R Mill Company, Inc.
45 West First North
Smithfield, Utah 84335
Corona flour mills.

Lee Engineering Co.
2023 West Wisconsin Avenue
Milwaukee, Wisconsin 53201
Electric flour mills.

FOOD SOURCES (ORGANIC)

Walnut Acres
Penns Creek, Pennsylvania 17862
One of the oldest and best organic farms in the country. Write for a mail-order catalog.

New Age Foods
1122 Pearl
Boulder, Colorado 80302
Health foods, vitamins, herbs—a reliable, good-hearted, caring source. Mail orders gladly filled.

American Tea & Spice
1511 Champa Street
Denver, Colorado 80202
  Staple foods and spices.

Organic Directory, a periodical
Rodale Press
Emmaus, Pennsylvania 18049
  An up-to-date listing of organic growers.

FOOD STORAGE PLAN

Perma-Pak
40 East 2430 South
Salt Lake City, Utah 84115
  Completely balanced dehydrated foods for storage and books about
  storage.

GRAINS

Ted A. Whitmer & Son
Bloomfield, Montana 59315
  Wheat.

HERBS

Nature's Herb Company
281 Ellis Street
San Francisco, California 94102
  Herbs and spices of all kinds; an old company with an interesting
  catalog.

HOME AND HOMESTEAD SUPPLIES OF ALL KINDS

Good Karma Looms
440-N West 4th
Chadron, Nebraska 69337
  Handcrafted heirloom-quality handlooms and spinning wheels
  by mail. Each piece lovingly made; every speck of sawdust goes
  on the compost heap.

Mother's Truck Store
Box 75
Unionville, Ohio 44088
Free catalog lists most of the tools needed for nitty gritty living—from root beer extract to coal and wood stoves to butter churns.

Montgomery Ward mail-order catalog
Sears Roebuck mail-order catalog
Most conventional tools needed around the house or homestead. Farm catalogs are free; orders are necessary to get on general catalog mailing list. There's generally a mail-order service in every area.

INFORMATION

County and Home Extension Agents
Each county throughout the U.S. has a County Extension Agent or Home Extension Agent who offers free information and booklets. Usually listed under "(Your county) County Government" in the phone book.

LIVESTOCK AND DAIRY SUPPLIES

American Supply House
Box 1114
Columbia, Missouri 65201
Supplies for dairy goats and sheep. Some cheese-making supplies.

SEEDS AND SPAWN

Gurney Seed & Nursery Company
Yankton, South Dakota 57078
Seeds, nursery stock, mushroom spawn.

TEAS

Celestial Seasonings, Inc.
Box 1405
Boulder, Colorado 80302
Fine teas like famous Red Zinger. Operated by glowing people, this growing group began by gathering herbs in our local forests,

now imports world-widely. Beth Hay, *Nitty Gritty Foodbook's* artist, does the packages and herb charts. Celestial Seasonings is searching for organic farmers who would like to grow herbs on contract for them.

UTENSILS

Earthly Goods
940 Pearl
Boulder, Colorado 80302
  Handles the "Happy Baby Food Grinder" and the finest cooking and kitchenware.

National Presto Industries
  Eau Claire, Wisconsin 54701
    Pressure cookers, canners, and replacement parts.

Montgomery Ward and Sears Roebuck
  Canning equipment of all kinds.

Ladle and Spoon

SUGGESTED READING

Starred items (*) are those most emphatically suggested by the author.

ANGIER, BRADFORD. *Gourmet Cooking for Free.* Harrisburg, Pa.: Stackpole Books, 1970. 190 pp.

*———. *One Acre and Security.* New York: Vintage Books, 1973. 320 pp. Good homesteading information.

ARNOLD, SAM. *Sam Arnold's Frying Pans West Cookbook.* 1969. Published by Sam Arnold, The Fort, Morrison, Colorado 80465. 50 pp. Includes information about frontier and native American cookery.

*BALL BROTHERS. *Ball Blue Book.* Muncie, Ind.: Ball Brothers Company, 1969. 100 pp. Top-notch canning information.

BATCHELOR, WALTER D. *Gateway to Survival Is Storage.* 1968. Published by Walter D. Batchelor, 6120 East Boston Street, Mesa, Arizona 85205. 34 pp. An excellent guide to food storage preparedness.

BENHAM, JACK, and SARAH BENHAM, *Rocky Mountain Receipts and Remedies.* 1966. Published by The Benhams, 489 Tejon Drive, Grand Junction, Colorado 81501. 58 pp. Frontier cookery and hints.

*Boy Scout Merit Badge Books. Boy Scouts of America. North Brunswick, New Jersey 08902. Simple, clear information.

Brooklyn Botanic Garden. *Gardening in Containers—A Handbook*, 1958. 80 pp. *Handbook on Herbs*, 1972. 93 pp. Brooklyn Botanic Garden, 1000 Washington Avenue, Brooklyn, New York 11225.

BURT, CALVIN P., and FRANK G. HEYL. *Edible and Poisonous Plants of the Eastern States* and *Edible and Poisonous Plants of the Western States*. 1970. Plant Deck, Lake Oswego, Oregon 97034. A color deck of 52 wild plant identification cards. The handiest guide I know of.

CHASE, A. W. *Dr. Chase's Recipes, or Information for Everybody*. 385 pp. Reprint of the original 1866 edition from Favorite Recipes Press, Inc., P. O. Box 18324, Louisville, Kentucky 40218. Contains valuable information about how to make and do just about everything—paint, yeast, tanning solutions, etc.

A Complete Guide to Home Meat Curing. Morton Salt Company, P. O. Box 355, Argo, Illinois 60501.

Cornell Home Economics Extension. *Quantity Recipes*. State College of Human Ecology, Mailing Room, Bldg. 7, Research Park, Cornell University, Ithaca, New York 14850. Recipes for large groups.

Countryside and Small Stock Journal, Rt. 1, Box 239 M, Waterloo, Wisconsin 53594.

*DAVIS, ADELLE. *Let's Cook It Right*. New York: New American Library, 1970. 574 pp.

———. *Let's Eat Right*. New York: New American Library, 1970. 534 pp.

———. *Let's Get Well*. New York: New American Library, 1972. 476 pp.

———. *Let's Have Healthy Children*. New York: New American Library, 1972. 382 pp.

DE BAIRACH LEVY, JULIETTE. *Nature's Children*. New York: Warner Paperback Library, 1971. 180 pp. A beautifully written book about raising children naturally.

DICKEY, ESTHER. *Passport to Survival*. Salt Lake City: Bookcraft Publishers, 1969. 180 pp. An excellent book about food preservation and storage.

*EWALD, ELLEN BUCHMAN. *Recipes for a Small Planet*. New York:

Ballantine Books, 1973. 371 pp. Cooking high-protein meals without meat.

*Farm Journal Freezing and Canning Cookbook. Garden City, New York: Doubleday and Company, 1964. 350 pp.

*GIBBONS, EUELL. Stalking the Good Life. New York: David McKay Company, 1971. 248 pp.

―――. Stalking the Healthful Herbs. New York: David McKay Company, 1973. 316 pp.

―――. Stalking the Wild Asparagus. New York: David McKay Company, 1970. 316 pp.

GROUT, ROY A. The Hive and the Honey Bee. Hamilton, Ill.: Dadant and Sons, 1963. 556 pp.

HATFIELD, AUDREY WYNNE. How to Enjoy Your Weeds. New York: Collier Books, 1973. 295 pp.

HENRICK, U. P. Sturtevant's Edible Plants of the World. New York: Dover Publications, 1972. 693 pp.

*HERTZBERG, RUTH; BEATRICE VAUGHAN; and JANET GREENE. Putting Food By. Brattleboro, Vt.: Stephen Greene Press, 1973. 371 pp.

*Home Canning Book and How to Freeze Foods. 1971. Kerr Glass Manufacturing Company, Sand Springs, Oklahoma 74063. 57 pp.

Home Cheesemaking. American Supply House, Box 114, Columbia, Missouri 65201. Free catalog of other books about goats and goat products.

*KAINS, M. G. Five Acres and Independence. New York: Dover Publications, 1973. 400 pp. A necessary book for homesteaders.

*KAYSING, BILL. First Time Farmer's Guide. 1971. Straight Arrow Books, 625 Third Street, San Francisco, California 94107. 320 pp. Great homesteading information.

KENDA, MARGARET ELIZABETH, and PHYLLIS S. WILLIAMS. The Natural Baby Food Cookbook. New York: Avon Publishers, 1972. 170 pp.

*KOLLIN, RICHARD. Super Index to The Mother Earth News. 1972. Richard Kollin, P.O. Box A, Willits, California 95490.

*LAPPÉ, FRANCES MOORE. Diet for a Small Planet. New York:

Ballantine Books, 1971. 301 pp. Principles of eating low on the food chain.

LUCAS, RICHARD. *Nature's Medicines.* New York: Award Books, 1966. 251 pp.

MCILVAINE, CHARLES and ROBERT K. MACADAM. *One Thousand American Fungi.* New York: Dover Publications, 1973. 729 pp. The comprehensive book of fungi, but a shortage of good color pictures.

*MARKS, VIC, ed. *Cloudburst, A Handbook of Rural Skills and Technology.* 1973. Cloudburst Press, Box 79, Brackendale, British Columbia, Canada. 128 pp.

*MARTIN, ALEXANDER C. *Weeds.* New York: Golden Press, 1972. 160 pp. Wild plants are viewed as weeds, but this book serves as a tremendous color-identification guide for wild edible plants.

MEYER, JOSEPH E. *The Herbalist.* New York: Sterling Publishing Co., 1968. 308 pp.

The Mother Earth News. P. O. Box 70, Hendersonville, North Carolina 28739. Good information for those developing an independent way of life.

The Mother Earth News Almanac. New York: Bantam Books, 1973. 373 pp.

*OLSON, LARRY DEAN. *Outdoor Survival Skills.* Provo, Utah: Brigham Young University Press, 1973. 188 pp. Survival skills, including foraging for plants and animals. Color plates of wild edible plants.

Organic Gardening and Farming magazine staff, CAROL STONER, ed. *Stocking Up.* Emmaus, Pennsylvania: Rodale Press, 1973. 351 pp.

The Purina Hog Book. Purina Company. Free at most feed stores.

Rabbits. Carnation Albers Company. Free at most feed stores.

Raising Better Livestock. Carnation Albers Company. Free at most feed stores.

Rodale Press. Emmaus, Pennsylvania 18049:
   The Encyclopedia of Organic Gardening
   Organic Gardening Magazine

*ROMBAUER, IRMA S., and MARION ROMBAUER BECKER. *Joy of*

Cooking. Indianapolis: Bobbs-Merrill Company, 1964. 850 pp. An excellent everyday book of recipes. (Also in paperback.)

SHUTTLEWORTH, FLOYD S. *Nonflowering Plants.* New York: Golden Press, 1967. 159 pp. Good introduction to mushrooms.

SLEIGHT, JACK, and RAYMOND HULL. *Home Book of Smoke Cooking Meat, Fish and Game.* Harrisburg, Pa.: Stackpole Books, 1971. 160 pp.

SMITH, ALEXANDER H. *The Mushroom Hunter's Field Guide.* Ann Arbor: University of Michigan Press, 1963. 368 pp.

STAMM, G. W. *Veterinary Guide for Farmers.* New York: Hawthorn Books, 1963. 384 pp.

*United States Department of Agriculture, Government Printing Office, Washington, D.C. 20402:
    Write the USDA for a complete listing of publications available. Most are free from local extension offices.

*United States Department of Agriculture. *Cheeses of the World.* New York: Dover Publications, 1972. 150 pp. Cheese recipes.

*————. *Complete Guide to Canning, Preserving and Freezing.* New York: Dover Publications, 1973. 214 pp. Includes all government publications on canning and freezing foods.

University of Alaska, Cooperative Extension Service, College, Alaska 99701. *Tanning at Home, 1971, # 320.*

The Whole Earth Catalog series.

WIENER, MICHAEL. *Earth Medicine, Earth Foods.* New York: Collier Books, 1972. 214 pp. Excellent material on wild edible food plants and herbs, and medicinal herbs.

FINIS.

INDEX

249

ILLUSTRATION CREDITS

Woodcuts and engravings reproduced throughout the book, unless otherwise noted below, are taken from: **1800 Woodcuts by Thomas Bewick and His School,** ed. Blanche Cirker (New York: Dover Publications, 1962); Bowles and Carver, **Catchpenny Prints** (New York: Dover Publications, 1970); **Happy Children** (New York and Chicago: Donohue Brothers, n.d.); and Clarence P. Hornung, **Handbook of Early Advertising Art,** 3d ed. (New York: Dover Publications, 1956). Drawings, unless otherwise noted below, are by Beth Hay. The illustrations on pages 40, 41, 43, and 45 are taken from U.S. Department of Agriculture, "Common Weeds of the United States" (New York: Dover Publications, 1971). The illustration on page 54 is taken from "How to Make Cheese on the Farm," ©Chr. Hansen's Lab, Inc., Milwaukee, Wisconsin. The illustration on page 111 is taken from Francis M. Lappé, **Diet for a Small Planet** (New York: Ballantine Books, 1971). The illustration on page 140 is taken from "Home Canning of Fruits and Vegetables," **Home and Garden Bulletin,** No. 8, U.S. Department of Agriculture. The illustration on page 141 is taken from "Canning Colorado Fruit," **Colorado State University Extension Bulletin,** No. 435-A. The illustration on page 149 is taken from "Take Care of Pressure Canners," Bureau of Human Nutrition and Home Economics, U.S. Department of Agriculture. The illustrations on page 166 (top, center) are taken from "Storing Vegetables and Fruits," **Home and Gardening Bulletin,** No. 119, U.S. Department of Agriculture. The illustration on page 166 (bottom) is taken from M.G. Kains, **Five Acres and Independence** (New York: Dover Publications, 1973). The illustrations on pages 170 and 171 are courtesy of Gurney Seed and Nursery Co., Yankton, South Dakota 57078. The illustration on page 227 is taken from "Processing and Marketing Farm Poultry," **Bulletin,** No. 7, U.S. Department of Agriculture.

ABOUT THE AUTHOR

SHERYLL PATTERSON HERDT spends much of her time on a recently acquired farm in Nebraska with her three children and large numbers of goats, chickens, dogs, and cats. She is preparing two books: *The Homestead Way of Life,* a study of self-sufficient American homesteads at the turn of the century, and *Life During the Great Depression,* on innovation and survival in America during the 1930s.